"The One Page Business Plan
does something outrageous!
It causes very busy people
to stop and think.
As they start to write...
it confirms both their clarity
and their confusion!"

— Jim Horan
President
The One Page Business Plan Company

WARNING – DISCLAIMER

This book was designed to provide information in regard to the subject matter covered. It is not the purpose of this manual to reprint all of the information available to the author/publisher, but to complement, amplify and supplement other sources.

Use of The One Page Business Plan® does not in any way guarantee the success of an idea or organization, nor does it ensure that financing will be made available. When legal or expert assistance is required, the services of a competent professional should be sought.

The author/publisher shall have neither liability nor responsibility to any person or entity with respect to any loss or damage caused, or alleged to be caused, directly or indirectly by the information contained in this book.

If you do not wish to be bound by the above, you may return this book to the publisher for a full refund.

Published by:

The One Page Business Plan Company
1798 Fifth Street
Berkeley, CA 94710
Phone: (510) 705-8400
Fax: (510) 705-8403
www.onepagebusinessplan.com

ISBN-13: 978-1-891315-05-3
ISBN-10: 1-891315-05-6

FIRST EDITION - v.1.2

Book Design by: Melodie Lane
Cover design by: Jim McCraigh
Edited by: Rebecca Salome Shaw

Printed in the United States of America

The One Page Business Plan®

*The Fastest, Easiest Way
to Write a Business Plan!*

By Jim Horan

Financial Services Edition

We Have a Rich History with Financial Advisors

Financial service professionals have been successfully writing One Page Business Plans since 1994.

There is a long list of individual agents, advisors, brokers, specialists, field leaders, sales executives, agency owners and managing partners who have successfully used The One Page Business Plan to create a focused and disciplined approach to growing their practice or business to the next level. Most claim this process does for them, what they do for their clients... it helps them prepare for the future by creating a clear, concise plan.

The list of professions using this process is long and wide; it includes: bankers, mortgage brokers, insurance agents (life, property & casualty, long-term care, business), stock brokers, financial planners, financial advisors, employee benefit brokers/advisors, estate planning attorneys and high net worth family advisors.

Companies or their agents using The One Page Business Plan include:

AIG	Marsh Inc.
Allstate Insurance	Massachusetts Mutual
Ameriprise Financial	MetLife
AXA Equitable	Morgan Stanley
Bank of America	Navitas, Ltd.
Capital Insurance Group	New York Life Insurance Company
Capital Planning Specialists	Northstar Financial
Chela Education Financing	Northwestern Mutual Life Insurance
Community Trust Bank	Old Republic Home Protection
Edward Jones	Principal Financial Group
Farmers Insurance Group	Private Capital Group
Fidelity Investments	The Mony Group
GAMA International	Thrivent Financial for Lutherans
Genworth Financial	Transamerica Life Insurance
Guardian Life Insurance Company	State Farm Insurance Companies
Guardian Trust Company	Sun Life Financial Canada
Heritage Bank	Waddell & Reed Financial Advisors
International Order of Foresters	Western America Mortgage
John Hancock Financial Network	Wells Fargo Bank

Industry Leaders Offer Sage Advice...

Know your vision! Be clear about what your practice will look like and be precise about who you want to serve. Know your critical numbers... the numbers that will make your practice successful. And be extraordinarily clear about why these numbers are important to you. Money by itself is not compelling enough to sustain you in this business. What's critical to an advisor's success? Face-to-face time with prospects. Million Dollar Roundtable qualifiers spend about 20% of each week with prospects; Top of Table Producers spend 50% of their time face-to-face. Invest in people, processes and technology that maximize your face-to-face time. Treat your practice as a business. Remember: If you can measure it, you can manage it! And when your values are clear, decisions are easy.

Edward Deutschlander, CLU, CLF
Executive Vice President, North Star Resource Group
President, GAMA International 2007 - 2008

You cannot run a financial practice by the seat of your pants... get focused and stay focused. Have a plan and a system. Execute it consistently! Don't let a little or a lot of success allow complacency to set in. Keep working your system through the highs and lows. Never forget the STP Principle: See The People! You cannot solve anybody's financial issues or sell them anything unless you spend time with them. Far too many new advisors will not call people because they are fearful they will be bothering them. Pick up the phone; everyone wants to have a substantive dialog about what is important to them. And never forget... selling is 90% listening. Be prepared to ask substantive questions.

Herman Dixon, CLU, CLF, LTCP, MBA
State Farm Agency Field Executive, Charleston, VA

Activity Activity Activity! You guarantee success in this industry by seeing people... consistently seeing people! See five to six new people a week, open four Fact-Finders and achieve a 50% close rate; you will have a very long, successful career. Too frequently new associates get bogged down trying to become technically proficient... instead of focusing on getting in front of new people. Develop your people skills. Learn how to find out what's really important to the people you are in front of and you have mastered one of the most important skills in this industry. As you learn the profession, your team can backfill any of the technical knowledge you are missing.

Timothy Murray, CLU, ChFC
Managing Director, John Hancock Financial Network, Cincinnati, OH
Past President, GAMA International 2006 - 2007

Most advisors don't understand they are not a salesman; they are the business owner. They need to treat their book of business as a business, even if they are an employee. It is absolutely critical they have a plan that defines their target customer. Failure to do so means they will be chasing too many opportunities. The most successful advisors focus on a particular niche, create a team of specialists and become extraordinarily efficient. The market is demanding credibility and confidence, specialization is critical for long term success.

Jeff Hughes
Chief Executive Officer, GAMA International
Washington, DC

More Sage Advice from Advisors...

Ideally, anyone coming into this business knows who they want to work with; unfortunately most don't. Therefore, in the early years, the new kids need to put in the hours; they flat need to just grind it out until they get very clear and specific about who they want to work with... then it begins to get easier. Get well known in your community; be active and volunteer. People buy financial services from people they know, like and trust. Be careful when older, more successful advisors give you clients they no longer want to work with... frequently they are not worth the effort. Keep your business simple; my favorite rule is the more complicated it is, the further away from it you should stay.

Ralph Miljanich
Associate Vice President, Morgan Stanley
Santa Cruz, CA

Master fact-finding and listening skills. I forget who said "selling ain't telling, it's listening". Whatever your area of specialization is, learn how to ask questions that allow the prospect to think and explain their situation as thoroughly as possible. Don't even begin to describe the solution you're thinking of until you both agree on their current situation, the problems encountered, the impact the problems are creating and the benefit, or need-payoff, the best solution will provide.

Rob Ferguson
Ferguson Associates Insurance & Financial Services, LLC
Walnut Creek, CA

Success: It's always about clarity and execution. Never engage in any selling or marketing effort unless you have a crystal clear goal in mind - what you will accomplish and when you will accomplish it. And always have a plan of action which includes your fundamental tools for getting the job done and the specific strategies you will follow. Ad-libbing is for amateurs!

Nick Ray, CLU, RHU, ChFC, MBC
Business Coach to Senior Financial Advisors
Berkeley, CA

Far too many advisors get caught in the busy trap. Compliance, meetings and paperwork can eat up valuable client face time. Invest in people and systems that allow you the maximum amount of time with prospects and clients. Also, the future is very limited as a lone ranger. Develop a team that consists of a rainmaker, fact finder, someone who does the case development and analysis and complete the team with someone that excels at the final presentation and can close. This is a formula for success!

Machen MacDonald, CPCC, CCSC
President, ProBrilliance!, Advisors to Independent Financial Advisors
Grass Valley, CA

Thirty years ago I went from a clerk to a Wall Street Trader in three years. I had very specific goals and worked my plan consistently. Today, as an advisor to financial brokers, advisors and agents my best advice is to 1) develop a specific niche, 2) get other people to market for you, by marketing for them, 3) become the "financial go-to-person" for your clients and 4) no matter what anyone else says -- never, ever, give up on your goals!

Maria Marsala
Business Strategist, Author, Speaker and former Wall Street Trader
Poulsbo, WA

and Senior Financial Executives

You don't get to the top of Mount Everest by wandering around and you won't have a successful career in financial services by wandering around. You need a good business plan and you need a solid model week. Manage your time by designing a model week that properly allocates time to essential marketing, sales and administrative activities. Engage your mental focus, emotional energy and time to execute on the activities that will make you successful. A career in financial services is like a basketball game... some score points and some just dribble. Commitment to a strong business plan coupled with a clear model week will help you to score in life and in your career!

Diane M. Ruebling
President, The Ruebling Group LLC
Former Group VP, American Express Financial Advisors
Scottsdale, AZ

Here are two pieces of advice for those who want to be successful in the financial services industry over the long run. First, over forty years ago I learned it was critical to have a solid opener. I knew precisely what I was going to say for the first fifteen minutes when I was with a new prospect. Ad-libbing is for amateurs. It is critical not to waste your time or the prospects time. Make it easy for the prospect to say no at anytime. Second piece of advice; master the art of selling fees. The transparency that hit the mutual fund industry twenty years ago is now bearing down on the rest of the financial industry. People that are not adept at selling fees will not be successful.

Dick Buxton, ChFC
Senior Managing Director, Private Capital Corp., Specialists in Stock Ownership Plans
Novato, CA

Rookies worry about the wrong things. Selling financial service products is not about the specifics of the products or services. In fact, most clients never really understand the products they are buying... they are way too complex. People buy financial products from people they trust... they have to - the process and products are too overwhelming. The pros spend quality time and money on their existing clients. They never rush them. Well served clients build incredible practices.

Chuck Longanecker
President, Business Development Systems
Sacramento, CA

The most successful and profitable financial advisors - registered investment advisors, independent broker dealers, insurance general agents - focus on segmentation. By focusing on a niche, whether it be age, wealth segment or vocation (i.e. airline pilots, retired government workers, etc.), they increase referrals, decrease competition, and generally have lower costs to serve their client base. With specialization, there are many effiences, for example, you only need to learn the benefit payout options for the pilots retirement plan once. Find the niche that works for you... and work it!

Neal Ringquist, President
Advisor Software, Inc.
Lafayette, CA

Foreword

What the world's leading author of business best-sellers is saying about The One Page Business Plan®...

"The One Page Business Plan is an out-and-out winner. Period.

It makes great sense to me as a so-called business thinker. But the acid test was applying it to a start-up I co-founded. We spent several days drafting our one pager - and have been editing it ever since. It is a powerful, living document; the very nature of which has led us to important new insights.

The One Page Business Plan = the proverbial better mouse trap!"

- Tom Peters
author of
Leadership,
Re-imagine!,
In Search of Excellence,
Thriving on Chaos,
The Pursuit of Wow!,
and The Circle of Innovation

What Others Are Saying

The One Page Business Plan® takes a complex process and makes it simple!

For years my annual business plan consisted simply of a set of objectives. The one-page business plan format forced me to think through each objective and create a strategy and action steps that align with the objectives and strategies. The web-based tracking form brought clarity to my results. Along with the vision and mission statement, the one-page plan is concise yet comprehensive in capturing the critical elements of accomplishing your goals.

Jeff Plummer
Associate Managing Partner, Carolinas General Agency, John Hancock Financial Network
Charlotte, NC

The One Page Business Plan uniquely simplifies the complex. It motivates, it focuses, and it inspires all on one page. The user friendly format makes this a necessary tool for any professional desiring to plan and build success.

Ryan Beck, CFP
Executive Vice President, AXA Advisors, LLC
Salt Lake City, UT

One Page Business Planning brought coordinated planning and organization to our diverse holdings of financial service companies; it has given us a common language and culture.

Bob Esperti
Chairman & CEO, QA3
Tucson, AZ

If there is no plan, there is chaos. The One Page Business Plan looks deceptively simple, but it is in fact an incredibly effective process that creates orderly fashion and accountability out of chaos and dysfunctionality. One Page Plans clearly and concisely document the change that needs to happen.

Chuck Longanecker
President, Business Development Systems
Sacramento, CA

GAMA International used the One Page Plan process to turn a four inch stack of research, surveys and reports, first into a laser sharp five-year strategic plan, then one-year plans for every department and committee. Every financial service company and every advisor would benefit from running their business with this level of precision.

Jeff Hughes
Chief Executive Officer, GAMA International
Washington, DC

It is far too easy for a stockbroker to get wrapped up in the market and lose perspective that you are in business for yourself. In order to be successful for the long run, one must have a plan and The One Page Business Plan is a great tool! I have had a One Page Plan for 10 years... it has served me very well.

Ralph Miljanich
Sr. Vice President, Morgan Stanley
Santa Cruz, CA

*"You must
simplify.
You must make
the complex simple,
then you must
make it work."*

— I.M. Pei
Master Architect

Author's Note

The opportunities in the world of financial services continue to increase exponentially. The question is, which of these opportunities will you pursue?

This industry is growing, but also becoming more and more competitive and complex. Baby boomers represent a tremendous opportunity, but will require more help than their parents in making financial plans because they will live longer and the choices are more complex. Sales cycles may be longer and many prospects with money will demand to be educated before they sign on the dotted line. Increasing regulations, compliance and transparency make the selling and servicing more complex and time-consuming.

What are you going to do to be competitive? How are you going to manage the complexity?

You can choose to take your business one day at a time and be totally opportunistic, or you can choose to take a path of greater control and predictability. If you choose to be more deliberate about your future, you will be doing for yourself what you do for your clients… creating a plan!

The problem with most planning processes is that they are too complex… and they take too long!

You need a simple structure and process for capturing your thoughts about your business. We are going to help you!

This book was created specifically for you… a financial service professional. It is absolutely the fastest, easiest way to create a plan for a financial practice. Using the One Page Plan methodology, you do not have to start with a blank page. We have designed templates and included examples based on the thousands of One Page Business Plans that have been created by some of the most successful financial advisors in the industry over the last 16 years.

We think we have done a lot of the hard work for you. We are glad to be with you on this journey. Take your time, enjoy the process… and don't stop until your One Page Plan represents your best thinking. Then go execute your plan with confidence.

Jim Horan
Author, Consultant, Speaker

How to Use This Book and CD

The primary purpose of this book is to help you get your plan onto paper. It has been carefully crafted to capture the plan that is in your head.

Carry this book with you, write in it, use it as a container for capturing your thoughts as they occur. If you have multiple businesses, partners or managers, have them get their own copy.

It's not necessary to do all the exercises in this book. If you can write your One Page Business Plan by reviewing the samples — skip the exercises. They are there to help guide you through the process if you need help.

This book does not look like the typical business planning book — it isn't intended to. The exercises and examples are meant to stimulate you. The graphics and images are meant to guide you. If they look playful, be playful and explore. If they look analytical, be analytical and focused. The examples and samples are from real business plans. They are meant to show you how powerful a few words or a well-constructed phrase can be.

Do not underestimate the power of the questions that appear simple! They are simple by design. If you do not get an "aha" from them, have somebody ask you the questions. Important insights may begin to flow.

This book is divided into nine sections with the focus on the five elements of The One Page Business Plan. You can start anywhere. It's OK to jump around!

There are many different ways to use and interact with this book. Exercises can be done:

- by oneself

- with a planning partner (2 or more financial advisors)

- as a management team

- as a group

- at a retreat or conference

- with a licensed One Page Business Plan consultant

The Financial Services Tool Kit CD at the back of the book contains the One Page Business Plan templates, bonus exercises, budget worksheet, plus scorecards for monitoring and tracking your results.

Business Plan Myths

- All business plans are in writing.

- They must be long to be good.

- Their primary purpose is to obtain financing.

- It's easier for others to write business plans.

- You can and should do it by yourself.

- It takes six months, a significant amount of executive and staff's time, and expensive consultants.

- If completed, it will sit unused on a bookshelf.

- My practice is too small; business plans are for much bigger organizations.

- I know where I am taking my business; I do not need a written business plan.

- I can just pay for a consultant to write the plan for me; that will be good enough.

Let's dispel the myths…

Table of Contents

■ VISION
■ MISSION
■ OBJECTIVES
■ STRATEGIES
■ ACTION PLANS

Introduction

What is a One Page Business Plan?

"Planning is a process... not an event!

One Page Plans are living, changing, evolving documents!"

The One Page Business Plan is an innovative approach to business planning that captures the essence of any business, project or program on a single page using key words and short phrases.

Most companies use the process to create not only the company's overall plan, but to also create plans for each supporting department, project and program. Since the creation of The One Page Business Plan in 1994, over 250,000 companies have successfully used the process to bring structure, alignment and accountability to their organizations. Many of those were financial services firms.

The flexible methodology makes it possible for entrepreneurs, business owners, executives, managers and professionals in every organization to have a plan. The standard format makes it easy to review, compare and understand plans.

One Page Business Plans work because:

- Plans actually get documented
- Plans are understandable
- Plans are easy to write, easy to update
- Every manager or team has one

The process creates:

- Alignment
- Accountability
- Results

Our Observations...

Why One Page?

You are busy; your time is limited. You want to spend your time in front of prospects and clients, marketing and selling your services. You are action and results oriented. Most of us are not good at prose writing... it takes too long to write a well-written sentence, paragraph, page or chapter - and far too long to read. People need to be able to read a plan in about five minutes. They want the essence... the key points. Then they want to talk... to ask clarifying questions, come to agreement... and then take action.

Why Plan?

Some need to write plans to get funding... however, since few financial practices are fundable other than by friends and family, funding is not the primary reason advisors write plans. Most people write plans because they either want or need to achieve different or better results. Plans are blueprints; they describe what is going to be built, how it will be done, and by whom... and the results to be measured.

Why Written Plans?

The spoken word is too fluid; we have a tendency to ramble. When we speak, we almost never say it exactly the same way twice... frequently we forget to share some of the most important details... or spend too much time on the unimportant things. When we write, we choose our words more carefully. Writing takes time, usually much more than talk. The written word requires a higher level of mindfulness and attention to detail. The written word also produces a contract with yourself and others that can be reread, refined... a source for refection and mindful change if necessary.

Asking people simple questions... works!

People love to talk about their business! They can easily answer questions like, what are you building, what will your practice look like in three years, what has made your business successful to date, what are the critical practice development projects and programs you have underway or planned, what do you measure to know if you are on track... and of course, why does your business exist?

The Power is in 5 Key Questions!

Business plan terminology is problematic. Depending on where you went to school, and the companies/organizations you have worked for... the terms Vision, Mission, Objectives, Strategies and Plans probably mean something different to you than the person sitting next to you. We have learned that business planning "definitions" just don't work. We have refined our questions over 16 years with hundreds of thousands of business owners. The five questions we will teach you are simple, easy to remember and they will help get your business plan out of your head and onto paper.

About Planning Processes

Starting with a blank page wastes valuable time!

The examples and the fill-in-the-blank prompts are learning aids... designed to help you quickly learn and master the One Page Business Plan technique. We have learned that most people learn by seeing examples, so we give you lots of them.

The dreaded "writer's block" can easily be eliminated by the use of our proprietary fill-in-the-blank templates. They make the creation of any portion of your business plan easy. Use the fill-in-the-blank templates to quickly capture your thoughts and create the first draft. You will also find that the extensive list of templates can spark your thinking and make sure that you give consideration to your "total" business.

Everyone on your team can and should write a One Page Business Plan!

The number one issue business owners and executives share with us is that they need people to work on the right things... and achieve specific results! Partners complain they are not on the same page! There is a simple solution: have your partners, associates, strategic alliance partners, managers and paid staff create One Page Business Plans for their businesses, profit centers, departments, projects or programs. Do not assume they are executing your plan. Have them create their own!

Final Thought: Plans are important... Execution is critical!

Financial advisors invest in planning because they want and need results. Plans are valuable because they provide the blueprint for where you are taking your practice and how you will get there... but ultimately the plans are only as good as the execution. Establish processes such as the scorecard tracking and monthly progress reviews to monitor the implementation of your plans.

Business Plan Terminology is Confusing

There are no universally acceptable definitions to the terms Vision, Mission, Objectives, Strategies or Action Plans. How you use these terms depends entirely on what school you went to and what companies you have worked for. Many companies never successfully complete their business plans because they cannot agree on the basic terminology. We solved the problem!

We translated the five standard business plan elements into five simple and universal questions:

Vision: What are you building?

Mission: Why does this business exist?

Objectives: What results will you measure?

Strategies: How will you build this business?

Action Plans: What is the work to be done?

Writing a business plan for a department or program?

Modify the Mission and Strategy questions by replacing the word "business" with department or program:

Department Usage

Mission: Why does this department exist?

Strategy: How will you build this department?

Program Usage

Mission: Why does this program exist?

Strategy: How will you build this program?

Business Plans Can be Simple and Clean

The best way to understand The One Page Business Plan is to read one... One Page Business Plans can generally be read in about five minutes or less.

Portland Insurance Agency
Consolidated Agency Plan
FY2011

vision

Within the next three years grow the Greater Portland Insurance Agency into a $15 million agency system with three locations providing auto, property & casualty, life insurance and financial services to individuals, families and businesses that are concerned about being protected from the unpleasant and unexpected events of life.

---

mission

Prepare and Protect the Families and Businesses in our community!

---

objectives

- Increase total revenue from $8 to $10 million in FY2011.
- Add 2,000 new policies in 2011 generating $1.2 million in incremental revenue.
- Increase average annual premium from $500 to $550.
- Increase client retention rate from 88.35% to 91%.
- Increase # of average appointments per agent from 1.9 to 5 per week by April 30th.
- Increase close rate from 25% to 50% by June 30th.
- Increase life insurance referrals from 2 to 5 per week per agent.
- Hire 5 new agents by April 1st, additional 7 new agents by October 1st.

---

strategies

- Become locally known for excellence in "family & business insurance solutions".
- Build long term relationships w/ prominent bus. leaders - create consistent referral source.
- Maximize visibility by serving on community, non-profit, & professional boards.
- Mine existing client base for "A" clients; use seminar marketing system to find "B"clients.
- Strategic Mktng Alliances - align w/ CPAs, attorneys, auto dealers, real estate professionals.
- Sell thru education; use computer presentations to assure consistent message delivery.
- Staffing - hire professionals, provide quality training, 1:1 mentoring, reward Winners.
- Streamline all internal support & admin functions thru effective & smart use of technology.

---

action plans

- Implement agent incentive reward plan Jan. 15, 2011.
- Kickoff new agent search/hire process Feb. 1st; Training to begin April 15th.
- Contribute 1 article/month to Oregonian & Portland Tribune newspapers beginning Feb. 1st.
- Develop strat. relationship/Coop mktg program w/ major CPA firm & Law firm beg. 5/1.
- Conduct Credit Union member estate planning workshops every 8 weeks starting July 1st.
- Launch "Help a Non-Profit" initiative Sept. 30th.
- Re-launch High School Financial Program Oct. 1st.
- Move to new Portland Financial Center Nov. 1st.

- VISION
- MISSION
- OBJECTIVES
- STRATEGIES
- ACTION PLANS

Assessment

What's working? What's not?

"Too many people over plan and under execute.

Plan for what is critical... then execute the plan."

Intuitively you know the status of your financial services practice or company... but when was the last time you stopped and gave it a checkup? Took a real look under the hood?

This section has five 10 Point Assessments to help you quickly determine what is working in your practice, and what isn't. We've also included a 10 Point Personal Assessment for you to do a little personal checkup, if you so desire.

These assessments are designed to help you quickly take the pulse of your financial practice, which areas are strong, which aspects need attention. As with all of the exercises in this book, they are meant to be done quickly, relying on your intuition, state of mind and frankly, what is keeping you up at night and/or making you smile.

We encourage you not to overwork these assessments. In our workshops we give participants about five minutes to do the overall organizational assessment on page 22.

It's possible that not all of the categories on the 10 Point Assessments will apply to your practice, if so, you have two choices, 1) ignore those that do not apply; 2) modify the category to reflect an area of your practice that is critical to your success.

If you have an established financial practice you should find the Marketing, Sales, Closing, and Practice Management assessments helpful. If you don't understand all the categories or business processes listed, ask another member of your team or a trusted advisor... these are critical processes that you and your team will want to master.

As you work through your plan, be sure to come back to these assessments to ensure your plan addresses the key issues you identify here.

What's Working in Your Financial Services Practice?

Step 1: Rate each of these elements on a scale of 1 to 10; 1 = disaster, 10 = brilliantly successful
Step 2: On page 23 identify the key elements/issues that influenced your rating.
Step 3: On page 23 make note of what needs to be changed to correct the problem areas.

1. Marketing/Prospecting Processes	N/A	1	2	3	4	5	6	7	8	9	10
2. Referral Marketing System	N/A	1	2	3	4	5	6	7	8	9	10
3. New Client Acquisition	N/A	1	2	3	4	5	6	7	8	9	10
4. Closing Ratio & Sales Results	N/A	1	2	3	4	5	6	7	8	9	10
5. Client Service Systems	N/A	1	2	3	4	5	6	7	8	9	10
6. Practice Management Systems	N/A	1	2	3	4	5	6	7	8	9	10
7. Administrative Functions/Office Support	N/A	1	2	3	4	5	6	7	8	9	10
8. Professional Development & Designations	N/A	1	2	3	4	5	6	7	8	9	10
9. Compliance	N/A	1	2	3	4	5	6	7	8	9	10
10. Profitability/Cash Flow	N/A	1	2	3	4	5	6	7	8	9	10
Overall Assessment		1	2	3	4	5	6	7	8	9	10

Step 4: As you develop your plan, be sure to come back to this page to address the issues identified here.

THE ONE PAGE BUSINESS PLAN

Where are the Opportunities for Improvement?

In left column: Identify key issues or opportunities that influenced your assessment.
In right column: Brainstorm actions that can be taken to improve low ratings or maintain high ratings.

Key Issue or Opportunity	Action to Improve or Maintain

Example for New Client Acquisition:	
New Client Campaigns	More phone contact, less emphasis on collateral, more listening, offer better solutions

Your Marketing Program: What's Working?

Step 1: Rate each of these elements on a scale of 1 to 10; 1 = disaster, 10 = brilliantly successful
Step 2: On page 25 identify the key elements/issues that influenced your rating.
Step 3: On page 25 make note of what needs to be changed to correct the problem areas.

1. Profile of Ideal Client	N/A	1	2	3	4	5	6	7	8	9	10
2. Well-defined Marketing Niche	N/A	1	2	3	4	5	6	7	8	9	10
3. Well-defined Personal Brand	N/A	1	2	3	4	5	6	7	8	9	10
4. Compelling Product & Service Offerings	N/A	1	2	3	4	5	6	7	8	9	10
5. Effective Prospecting & Networking Systems	N/A	1	2	3	4	5	6	7	8	9	10
6. Client Referral Marketing System	N/A	1	2	3	4	5	6	7	8	9	10
7. Centers of Influence (COI)	N/A	1	2	3	4	5	6	7	8	9	10
8. Advertising, Promotions, Events, Seminars	N/A	1	2	3	4	5	6	7	8	9	10
9. Web Site and Other Collateral	N/A	1	2	3	4	5	6	7	8	9	10
10. Activity Tracking System	N/A	1	2	3	4	5	6	7	8	9	10
Overall Assessment		1	2	3	4	5	6	7	8	9	10

Step 4: As you develop your plan, be sure to come back to this page to address the issues identified here.

THE ONE PAGE BUSINESS PLAN

Where are the Opportunities for Improvement?

In left column: Identify key issues or opportunities that influenced your assessment.
In right column: Brainstorm actions that can be taken to improve low ratings or maintain high ratings.

Key Issue or Opportunity	Action to Improve or Maintain

Example for Advertising, Promos, Events:	
Local newspaper advertising producing too few leads	Move to more personal forms of business development like seminars & special events.

Your Sales Process: What's Working?

Step 1: Rate each of these elements on a scale of 1 to 10; 1 = disaster, 10 = brilliantly successful
Step 2: On page 27 identify the key elements/issues that influenced your rating.
Step 3: On page 27 make note of what needs to be changed to correct the problem areas.

1. Defined & Consistent Sales Process	N/A 1 2 3 4 5 6 7 8 9 10
2. Prospect Qualification/Needs Identification	N/A 1 2 3 4 5 6 7 8 9 10
3. Effective Fact Finder	N/A 1 2 3 4 5 6 7 8 9 10
4. Compelling Presentations & Proposals	N/A 1 2 3 4 5 6 7 8 9 10
5. Effective Use of Specialists	N/A 1 2 3 4 5 6 7 8 9 10
6. Ability to deal with Objections	N/A 1 2 3 4 5 6 7 8 9 10
7. Clearly Communicated Fee Structure	N/A 1 2 3 4 5 6 7 8 9 10
8. Future Opportunity Identification	N/A 1 2 3 4 5 6 7 8 9 10
9. Record/Track Sales Activities	N/A 1 2 3 4 5 6 7 8 9 10
10. Compliant Materials/Process	N/A 1 2 3 4 5 6 7 8 9 10
Overall Assessment	1 2 3 4 5 6 7 8 9 10

Step 4: As you develop your plan, be sure to come back to this page to address the issues identified here.

THE ONE PAGE BUSINESS PLAN

Where are the Opportunities for Improvement?

In left column: Identify key issues or opportunities that influenced your assessment.
In right column: Brainstorm actions that can be taken to improve low ratings or maintain high ratings.

Key Issue or Opportunity	Action to Improve or Maintain

Example for Fact Finder:

Current Fact Finder is not working; not producing the right discovery information	Collaborate with other advisors to refine Fact Finder to work with the 40 - 60 working trades population.

Your Closing Process: What's Working?

Step 1: Rate each of these elements on a scale of 1 to 10; 1 = disaster, 10 = brilliantly successful
Step 2: On page 29 identify the key elements/issues that influenced your rating.
Step 3: On page 29 make note of what needs to be changed to correct the problem areas.

1. Defined & Consistent Closing Process	N/A 1 2 3 4 5 6 7 8 9 10
2. Know When to Close	N/A 1 2 3 4 5 6 7 8 9 10
3. Consistently Confirm Prospect's Problem	N/A 1 2 3 4 5 6 7 8 9 10
4. Confirm Client Expectations	N/A 1 2 3 4 5 6 7 8 9 10
5. Discover/Confirm Client's Budget	N/A 1 2 3 4 5 6 7 8 9 10
6. Presentation of Solution	N/A 1 2 3 4 5 6 7 8 9 10
7. Consultation with all Decision Makers	N/A 1 2 3 4 5 6 7 8 9 10
8. Ability to Deal with Objections	N/A 1 2 3 4 5 6 7 8 9 10
9. Acceptance of Offer, Getting Started	N/A 1 2 3 4 5 6 7 8 9 10
10. Payment Process, Terms, Options	N/A 1 2 3 4 5 6 7 8 9 10
Overall Assessment	1 2 3 4 5 6 7 8 9 10

Step 4: As you develop your plan, be sure to come back to this page to address the issues identified here.

Where are the Opportunities for Improvement?

In left column: Identify key issues or opportunities that influenced your assessment.
In right column: Brainstorm actions that can be taken to improve low ratings or maintain high ratings.

Key Issue or Opportunity	Action to Improve or Maintain

Example for Dealing with Objections: Not dealing with objections effectively.	Explore how other advisors handle similar objections. Consider taking seminar. Getting mentor.

Practice Management: What's Working?

Step 1: Rate each of these elements on a scale of 1 to 10; 1 = disaster, 10 = brilliantly successful
Step 2: On page 31 identify the key elements/issues that influenced your rating.
Step 3: On page 31 make note of what needs to be changed to correct the problem areas.

1. Strong Administrative Support	N/A 1 2 3 4 5 6 7 8 9 10
2. Accounting Software & System	N/A 1 2 3 4 5 6 7 8 9 10
3. Contact & Client Management System	N/A 1 2 3 4 5 6 7 8 9 10
4. Proposal Software	N/A 1 2 3 4 5 6 7 8 9 10
5. Property & Casualty/Liability Insurance	N/A 1 2 3 4 5 6 7 8 9 10
6. Business Plan & Budget	N/A 1 2 3 4 5 6 7 8 9 10
7. Benefit & Retirement Programs	N/A 1 2 3 4 5 6 7 8 9 10
8. Computer Hardware/Software	N/A 1 2 3 4 5 6 7 8 9 10
9. Business Coach/Advisor/Consultant	N/A 1 2 3 4 5 6 7 8 9 10
10. Profitable & Cash Flow Positive	N/A 1 2 3 4 5 6 7 8 9 10
Overall Assessment	**1 2 3 4 5 6 7 8 9 10**

Step 4: As you develop your plan, be sure to come back to this page to address the issues identified here.

Where are the Opportunities for Improvement?

In left column: Identify key issues or opportunities that influenced your assessment.
In right column: Brainstorm actions that can be taken to improve low ratings or maintain high ratings.

Key Issue or Opportunity	Action to Improve or Maintain

Example for Admin Support: Buried in too much administrivia	Hire a part-time assistant to start; within 2 years, make a full-time position.

How are you? A Personal Assessment (optional)

Step 1: Rate each of these elements on a scale of 1 to 10; 1 = disaster, 10 = brilliantly successful
Step 2: On page 33 identify the key elements/issues that influenced your rating.
Step 3: On page 33 make note of what needs to be changed to correct the problem areas.

1. Your Physical Health	N/A	1	2	3	4	5	6	7	8	9	10
2. Your Mental Health	N/A	1	2	3	4	5	6	7	8	9	10
3. Relationships at Work	N/A	1	2	3	4	5	6	7	8	9	10
4. Your Role at Work	N/A	1	2	3	4	5	6	7	8	9	10
5. Personal Finances	N/A	1	2	3	4	5	6	7	8	9	10
6. Life Outside of Work	N/A	1	2	3	4	5	6	7	8	9	10
7. Sense of Community	N/A	1	2	3	4	5	6	7	8	9	10
8. Plans for Retirement	N/A	1	2	3	4	5	6	7	8	9	10
9. Stress Level	N/A	1	2	3	4	5	6	7	8	9	10
10. Sense of Well Being	N/A	1	2	3	4	5	6	7	8	9	10
Overall Assessment		1	2	3	4	5	6	7	8	9	10

Step 4: As you develop your plan, be sure to come back to this page to address the issues identified here.

Where are the Opportunities for Improvement?

In left column: Identify key issues or opportunities that influenced your assessment.
In right column: Brainstorm actions that can be taken to improve low ratings or maintain high ratings.

Key Issue or Opportunity	Action to Improve or Maintain

Example for Life Outside Work:

Not having enough fun! Need some downtime!

Consider taking Mondays off, or every other Monday. Need time to rejuvenate. Spend time on the boat with family.

VISION
MISSION
OBJECTIVES
STRATEGIES
ACTION PLANS

The Vision Statement
What are you building?

"If you don't get the words right...

you might build the wrong business!"

Everybody is building something... a company, an organization, a department, an independent practice. Well-written Vision Statements answer the question: What is being built?... in three sentences or less!

The question for you is what are you building? What do you want your financial services practice or company to look like in 1, 3 or 5 years? An effective Vision Statement need not be long, but it must clearly describe what you are building. A few key words will go a long way.

Vision Statements answer these questions:

- What type of company or practice is this?
- What markets does it serve?
- What is the geographic scope?
- Where will the business be located?
- Who are the target customers?
- What are the key products and services?
- How big will the company be?
- What will revenues be?
- Will it have employees? How many?

Almost everyone has a Vision for their company, but some are better at articulating it. Many people struggle with capturing their Vision effectively in writing. At The One Page Business Plan Company we have learned that with a little prompting, most business professionals, executives and owners can capture the essence of their Vision in just a few minutes.

Interview Exercise

Slightly overwhelmed? Want to make the process inclusive? Invite a trusted friend, colleague or advisor to interview you using the questions below. Have them interview you in person or over the phone. Have them ask you the questions and record your responses. You might consider doing this interview process with more than one person.

1. Who's the perfect client?

Describe three characteristics of the ideal recipient of your service/product:

Describe three characteristics of clients you would be better off NOT SERVING:

2. What's the service or product?

Describe three characteristics of your service or product:

Describe three things your service or product WON'T DO:

3. What's the competitive environment?

Describe three characteristics of successful financial service practices you admire and WOULD like to emulate:

Describe three characteristics of financial service professionals you WILL NOT emulate:

focus
EXERCISE

Crafting Your Vision Statement

Getting the first draft onto paper is always the most difficult. It is infinitely easier to edit! The fill-in-the-blank-template below is geared to help you quickly create a first draft. Each blank in essence is a question; complete all the blanks, and you create a first draft... quickly and easily! Not able to fill in all of the blanks at this time? Don't worry... complete those that you can! Revisit the blanks later, you may need to do some research or enlist help from others.

Vision Statement

Within the next _____ years grow _____ into a $_____
                                                    (company name)   (est. annual sales)

_____   _____ company providing
   (geographic scope)   (type of business)
   (local/region/nat'l/int'l)

_____
                        (list 2-3 of your key products/services)

to _____
                        (list 2-3 key clients/customers)

The following Vision Statement was created using the fill-in-the-blanks template and then edited. It is brief, but very clear.

> "Within the next <u>3</u> years grow <u>Roberta Jones' practice at Boston Financial Advisory Services</u> into a <u>regional</u> <u>financial advisory practice managing $40 million in assets yielding at least $350,000 in gross revenue</u> specializing in <u>plan development and asset management</u> for <u>professional working women age 30 to 60 who want to be financially prepared for retirement</u>."

VISION
MISSION
OBJECTIVES
STRATEGIES
ACTION PLANS

Mission

Why does this financial practice exist?

Mission Statements always answer the question, "Who will we serve and what will we do for them?"

Every company exists for a reason. Good Mission Statements describe why your product, service, department, project, program or business exists. Great Mission Statements are short and memorable. They communicate in just a few words (8 words are ideal) the company's focus and what is being provided to customers. They always answer the question, "Why will customers buy this product or service?"

Some of the best Mission Statements are an integral part of a company's branding strategy that compels customers to buy, but the same Mission Statements can and do direct and influence all significant business and management decisions.

For financial services professionals it is critical to have a Mission Statement that speaks to your ideal client... and to you. If your practice is built to serve first generation immigrant families, your Mission Statement should speak to them. If your ideal client is a high net worth executive in his early fifties, you will must have a Mission Statement that attracts them. Working with professional women in their thirties? Young couples just starting their careers? Businesses with 50–500 employees? Grandparents? You must have a Mission Statement that explains in 6–10 words how you help them with their financial matters.

Mission Statements answer these specific questions:

- Why does this business exist?
- What is our unique selling proposition?
- What are we committed to providing to our customers?
- What promise are we making to our clients?
- What wants, needs, desires, pain or problems do our product/services solve?

Use the fill-in-the-blank template below to create a first draft of your Mission Statement. Experiment with variations until you come up with a short, powerful, memorable statement that describes your ideal client and how you serve them.

Why does this financial practice exist?

1st Attempt:

We help _____ _____!
           (recipient of your services)   (goal or benefit of your services)

2nd Attempt:

3rd Attempt:

Examples of Mission Statements

The best Mission Statements are short and memorable! And eight words or less!

They also may evoke an emotional response through humor or the senses. Well written Mission Statements attract customers and also drive behavior within an organization.

As you review these Company Mission Statements, ask yourself how well do they answer the question, "Why does this company exist?"

The Investment Center	Help individuals and families fund higher education and protect retirement income and assets.
Tri-Valley Financial Advisory Services	We help families protect their families!
Tulsa Risk & Insurance Services	Create peace of mind through proactive personal risk management.
McKenzie Estate Planning Associates	We help create, preserve & utilize family wealth for important social causes.
Family Wealth Counselors, Inc.	We help families create, preserve and transfer their wealth.
Portland Insurance Agency	Prepare and protect the families and businesses in our community!
Memphis Financial Advisors	We help families achieve & maintain financial independence over multiple generations.
Chela Financial	We finance lifelong learning!
Nicola Nichol, UBS Financial Advisor	Provide financial peace of mind to every woman!

VISION
MISSION
OBJECTIVES
STRATEGIES
ACTION PLANS

Objectives

What will be measured?

"Be specific in your goal-setting! Use your goals to drive your behavior!"

Objectives are short statements that quantify the end results of any work effort. Good Objectives are easy to write and are instantly recognizable. They answer the question "What will we measure?"

Objectives clarify the results you want or need to accomplish in specific, measurable terms. For an Objective to be effective, it needs to be a well-defined target or outcome with quantifiable elements. It is important to include different types of Objectives that cover the entire scope of your professional practice or company.

Well conceived Objectives:

- Provide a quantitative pulse of the business
- Focus resources towards specific results
- Define success in a measurable manner
- Give people/organizations specific targets
- Establish a framework for accountability and incentive pay
- Minimize subjectivity and emotionalism
- Measure the end results of work effort

Although there is no magical number of Objectives, a One Page Business Plan can accommodate nine. Consider two to three Objectives for sales or revenue, one for profitability, two or three for marketing, one or two that are process oriented.

Objectives Must be Graphable

The One Page methodology makes writing Objectives simple: All Objectives must be graphable!

We learn early in our careers that what we measure is what gets improved. If you are serious about growing a profitable financial services practice or company that is cash flow positive, then chart your critical success factors. Have a chart for number of calls, appointments, referrals, closes, cases, billable days or hours, total revenues, assets under management, total premiums written, average sale, active client count, number of speaking engagements... whatever you know is critical for your success.

Charts are great... everybody can read charts. It's obvious when you are ahead of goal or not!

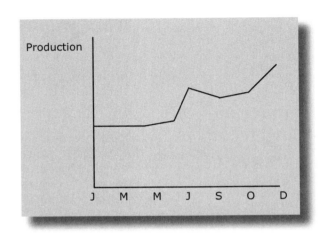

The key to setting meaningful Objectives is to identify goals that are:

- critical to your success and
- can be easily tracked
  (*Easily tracked = data is readily available and the specific target can be counted*)

Stated very simply, if you can not count it over time (easily)... it's not an Objective. On the Crafting Objectives exercise, we provide you with a number of frequently used goals in financial service practices and companies... please note, all of them are graphable!

It's easy to craft meaningful Objectives when you use these 3 simple guidelines:

- Write only Objectives that can be graphed
- Include a numerical value in every Objective
- Assign a name and date to assure accountability

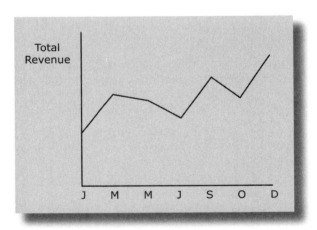

Excel template for scorecarding is on CD.

A Simple Formula for Writing Objectives...

> *Action To Be Taken*
> +
> *Something Countable*
> +
> *Target/Completion Date*

Here are examples for individual agent or advisors using this formula:

- Increase total personal income from $95,000 in 2010 to $150,000 in 2011.

- Add 30 new clients in 2011; 13 in 1st half, 9 in Q3, 8 in Q4.

- Increase total premiums written/GDC in 2011 from $600,000 to $1,000,000.

- Increase Assets under Management from $40 to $55 million by Dec. 31st.

- Increase number of open & active cases from 8 to 12 by August 31st.

- Give at least 8 seminars in 1st half 2011; 12 in 2nd half.

Examples for field leaders, sales executives, managing partners and agency owners:

- Increase total branch production from $3 to $4 million in FY2011.

- Add 2,000 new transactions generating $1.2 million incremental production credit in 2011.

- Increase client retention from 88.35% to 91% by year end.

- Recruit 20 new advisors by June 30th.

- Increase average advisor income from $125,000 to $160,000 by year end.

- Acquire additional 250 financial planning clients by Sept. 30th.

- Recruit 10 new advisors to increase branch size from 45 to 55 by Oct 31st.

Crafting Your Objectives

Listed below are templates for Objectives that are frequently used in the financial services industry. They are designed to help you quickly create a first draft. Keep in mind the industry includes many diverse segments: life insurance, annuities, stocks/equities, bonds, fee-based planners... and many more.

Financial

Total Income/Production
Achieve 2011 total income/sales/revenue/production of $ _____.

Commissions Earned
Increase commissions earned from $ _____ to $ _____.

Fees earned
Increase _____ fees earned from $ _____ to $ _____.

Operating & Marketing Expenses
Increase (decrease) Oper. & Mktg. Exp. from $_____ to $_____ (or % of sales).

Profit (revenues less expenses)
Increase pre-tax profits from $ _____ to $ _____ in 2011 (or % of sales).

Customer

New or Active Clients
Increase number of new/active clients from _____ to _____ by _____.

Units, Cases, Policies Sold, Assets under Management
Increase number of _____ sold from _____ to _____.

Average Production/Revenue per Sale
Increase average revenue per sale from $ _____ to $ _____.

Workshops/Programs/Special Events/Seminars
Conduct at least _____ workshops in 2011 w/ average attendance of _____ per event.

Retention/Renewals/Repeat Business
Increase percent of sales made to existing clients from _____% to _____%.

It is unlikely all of these templates will be appropriate for your practice or firm. If you do not see a template for an Objective that you need, create your own using the others as a model. For more options see pages 48 - 49.

Process Improvement*

Ideal Referrals
Increase # of ideal referrals received per month from _____ to _____ by _____.

Centers of Influence/Network Referrals
Increase # of COI/Network referrals received per month from _____ to _____.

Contacts/Appointments/Presentations
Increase # of _____ per week from _____ to _____ by _____.

Fact Finders Completed
Increase # of Fact Finders completed per week from _____ to _____ by _____.

Closing Ratio
Increase closing ratio from _____% to _____% by _____.

*Process Improvement for Marketing, Sales, Client Services and Administrative processes

Learning & Growth

Skill Improvement
Increase # of CE/training days from _____ to _____.

Resource Utilization
Improve _____ (resource) utilization from _____ to _____.

Output per Advisor/Employee
Increase _____ per advisor/employee from _____ to _____ by _____ (date).

Waste/Inefficiencies*
Reduce _____ waste from $ _____ to $ _____ by _____ (date).

Achievement
Have _____% of advisors/employees achieve _____% of goals.

*Wasted time, unnecessary travel, expensive meals & entertainment, etc.

More Objectives...

On these two pages are another set of templates designed around the core business development processes of Marketing/Prospecting and Revenue/Sales/Production. These lists are more expansive and provide more choices for your consideration as you are developing your plan. Reminder: Your One Page Plan has the capacity for a total of nine Objectives. We also include some Personal/Well-Being Objectives for consideration.

Marketing/Prospecting

Contacts
Increase # of contacts per day from _____ to _____ by _____.

Appointments
Increase # of appointments per day from _____ to _____.

Presentations
Increase # of presentations per week from _____ to _____.

Closes
Increase # of closes per week from _____ to _____.

New Clients
Increase # of ideal clients from _____ to _____.

Public Speaking
Give at least _____ presentations in 1st half of 2011; _____ in 2nd half.

Publishing/Articles
Commit to writing _____ articles per quarter in 2011.

Special Events
Increase # of special events from _____ to _____ by _____.

Seminars/Educational Events
Increase # of seminars/workshops from _____ to _____ by _____.

Tradeshows/Conventions
Generate _____ prospects by attending _____ tradeshows/conventions in 2011.

Direct Mail Programs
Increase # of direct mail programs from _____ to _____ by _____.

Prospect Calling
Increase calling activity per week from _____ to _____ by _____.

COI - Center of Influence
Increase # of active COI's from _____ to _____. Meet with _____ COI's per month.

Marketing, Sales and Personal

Revenue/Sales/Production

Income/Production per Month
Increase monthly income/production from $ _____ to $ _____ by _____.

Income/Production per Client
Increase income/production per client from $ _____ to $ _____ by _____.

Premiums Written
Increase total premiums written from $ _____ to $ _____.

Policies
Increase # of policies written from _____ to _____; Total premiums: _____.

Assets under Management
Increase Assets under Management from $ _____ to $ _____.

Product Sales
Increase _____ product sales from $ _____ to $ _____.

Project Sales
Sell _____ projects or engagements at $ _____ for a total of $ _____.

Cases
Increase # of open/active cases from _____ to _____ by _____.

Case Size
Increase average engagement from $ _____ to $ _____.

Earned Fees per Client
Increase average earned fees per client from $ _____ to $ _____.

Personal/Well-Being

Exercise
Increase exercise sessions per week from _____ to _____.

Weight
Decrease my weight from _____ to _____ by _____.

Vacation/Free Time
Commit to _____ weeks of vacation this year; _____ days of free time.

Community Service
Increase (decrease) total hours of community service from _____ to _____.

Personal Networth
Increase personal networth from $ _____ to $ _____ by _____.

Sample Objectives for Advisors/Agents...

Here are six sets of Objectives from six very different companies. In these examples there are 6 to 8 Objectives that describe "what these financial services firms will measure each month over the next 12 months to determine if they are on track."

Wealth Builders

- Increase assets under management from $15 to $25 million.
- Increase income after business expenses from $150,000 to $220,000 in 2011.
- Increase ROA from .85% to 1.0%.
- Increase average acct. from $250,000 to $600,000 in three years; $350,000 by Dec. 2011.
- Increase number of active accounts from 60 to 72 by year end.
- Volunteer 10 hours a month with the American Red Cross.
- Take a total of 30 days of vacation and free days in 2011.

Tri-Valley Financial Advisors

- Achieve 2011 Production growth of 67%. Grow from $150,000 to $250,000.
- Boost return on assets from 0.20% to 0.40%.
- Increase assets from $49 million to $60 million
- Hold total number of accounts constant while culling lowest 10% of accounts from my BOB.
- Decrease transaction-based revenues from 38% to 30%.
- Achieve $1 million in managed money by May 31st.
- Achieve pre-tax earnings of $135,000.

Denise Bounder, Financial Planning Services

- Increase Weighted Commission Credits (WCC) from 38,000 to 50,000 in 2011.
- Grow LAD (life, annuity, disability) business from $28,000 to $35,000.
- Secure two existing retirement plans, each w/ assets of at least $1 million by 8/30.
- Be at OC every Thursday to develop 10 new clients, generating $10,000 in revenue.
- Increase client base by 20, generating $20,000 in revenue.
- Secure introductions to 15 business owners in target market by 6/30.

and Field Leaders/Executives/Owners

Some of these Objectives are rather traditional, others are a little unique. We hope they will get you to think creatively about your business… and what counts!

Portland Insurance Agency

- Increase total revenue from $8 to $10 million in FY2011.
- Add 2,000 new policies in 2011 generating $1.2 million in incremental revenue.
- Increase average annual premium from $500 to $550.
- Increase client retention rate from 88.35% to 91%.
- Increase # of average appointments per agent from 1.9 to 5 per week by April 30th.
- Increase close rate from 25% to 50% by June 30th.
- Increase life insurance referrals from 2 to 5 per week per agent.
- Hire 5 new agents by April 1st, additional 7 new agents by October 1st.

The Financial Designers

- Increase estate planning service fees from $725,000 to $900,000 in FY2011.
- Acquire an additional 75 target clients with average estate of $2 million.
- Acquire 12 new clients with minimum net worth of at least $5 million each.
- Achieve 98% retention of recurring maintenance fees w/ existing clients.
- Create minimum of one media exposures per month, per community. Total exposures 150.
- Increase average fee per plan from $8,500 to $10,000.
- Increase total earnings per partner after expenses from $135,000 to $160,000.

Excel Financial Strategies, Inc.

- Increase gross revenues from $3.0 to $3.5 million in 2011.
- Increase net dividends from $500,000 to $700,000.
- Increase net profit margin from 20% to 30%.
- Increase consulting, planning & retainer fees from $100,000 to $150,000.
- Increase AUM held at MS from $315M to $385M.
- Increase reserve account from $150,000 to $200,000.
- Host 120 educational presentations, average 2 per month/partner.
- Increase average annual revenue per client from $4,200 to $5,000.

VISION
MISSION
OBJECTIVES
STRATEGIES
ACTION PLANS

Strategies

How will this business be built?

Success is rarely an accident. It is usually the result of executing a carefully crafted set of strategies. Strategies provide a blueprint or road map for building and managing a professional practice or a company. They also provide a comprehensive overview of the company's business model and frequently say as much about what the company will not do, as what it will do.

Strategies set the direction, philosophy, values, and methodology for building and managing your company. They establish guidelines and boundaries for evaluating business decisions. Following a predefined set of strategies is critical to keeping your professional practice on track.

One way of understanding strategies is to think of them as industry practices. The financial services industry has its leaders, its followers and its rebels; each has their own approach for capturing market share. Pay attention to the successful businesses and you can learn important lessons. You can also learn a lot from the failures.

Strategies are not secret. In fact, they are common knowledge and openly shared in the financial services industry. Pick up any financial services industry publication and you will know precisely what the industry's leaders have to say about the opportunities and how to capitalize on them. These leaders will also share their current problems and their solutions. This is critical information for building and managing your business. Capture the best thinking/best practices from the industry along with the strategies that make your professional practice or company unique and you will have a powerful set of strategies that drive your company forward!

In summary, Strategies are broad statements, covering multiple years that:

- Set the direction, philosophy, values
- Describe ideal clients, and how you will attract them
- Define your products, services and business model
- Establish guidelines for evaluating important decisions
- Set limits on what your company will do or will not do

Components of a
Successful Practice

There are many moving parts to a successful financial services practice. There are a lot of decisions to be made. Many of the decisions are personal preference.

Keep in mind that nobody gets all the parts and pieces in place before they start. It takes time, probably three to five years. Review this list; use it as a catalyst to think about what will actually be necessary to make your financial services practice successful over time. As you are crafting your Strategies on pages 58 and 59, refer to this page.

☐	Technical Knowledge	☐	Marketing & Sales Tracking Systems
☐	Professional Designations	☐	Client Service System
☐	Appropriate Licenses	☐	Professional website
☐	Strong Communication Skills	☐	Compliant Processes/Materials
☐	Presentation/Speaking Skills	☐	Practice Management Systems
☐	Well-defined Personal Brand	☐	Contact/Client Management System
☐	Well-defined Marketing Niche	☐	Business Plan & Budget
☐	Compelling Product/Service Offerings	☐	Business Office
☐	Networking & Prospecting Systems	☐	Computers, Software & Support
☐	Referral Marketing System	☐	Administrative Support
☐	Active COI (center of influence)	☐	Accounting System
☐	Effective Fact Finder	☐	Benefit/Retirement Programs
☐	Well Defined Sales Process	☐	Insurance Coverage
☐	Compelling Presentations	☐	Mentor/Coach/Advisor
☐	Clear & Compelling Proposals	☐	Family Support
☐	Clear & Understandable Fee Structure	☐	Peace of Mind
☐	Professional Advisory Team	☐	Free Time

Deciding Which Strategies Are Appropriate for Your Business:

Finding appropriate strategies for your business is not difficult. As you can see from the list above... there are many choices.

Much information is readily available to you for free or at minimal cost. There are multiple professional trade associations that serve your niche. Go online and explore. Ask other financial advisors/agents in your niche how to research the latest trends in your industry.

The key question is: which strategies will you select... and at what time in the life cycle of your practice or company. You cannot execute all of your strategies at the same time.

The most important strategy might be for you to become known as a source of referrals. Want referrals? Give them freely, regularly and make sure they are reciprocal.

Research Exercise

Review the last three issues of your industry's trade, professional or association journals and answer the questions below.

What and where are the opportunities?	How can you capitalize on them?

What threats exist?	How can you minimize the threats and/or turn them into opportunities?

Examples of Issues Affecting the Financial Services Industry

- Baby-Boomers represent a tremendous opportunity, but will need more help than their parents because they will live longer and the choices are more complex.

- Top producers will invest heavily & continuously in training.

- Major institutions are requiring advisors to do more of their own lead generation. Top producers will master marketing.

- Sales cycles may be longer; prospects with money will demand to be educated.

- Competitive pressures are reducing commission structures. Long term success requires ability to sell fees.

- Regulatory environment is bringing higher levels of transparency – which will require greater communication & educational skills.

A Simple Formula for Writing Strategies...

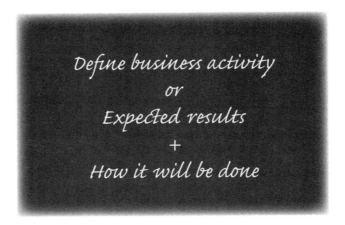

Define business activity
or
Expected results
+
How it will be done

Here are some examples using this formula:

Positioning   Become known for solving business succession issues by writing & speaking.

Perfect Client   Attract young families thru seminars, workshops & referrals.

Opportunities   Focus on aging Baby Boomers who are in a panic about their retirement.

**Products/
Services**   Specialize in fee-based plans; targeting women aged 40-60.

Initial Trial   Promote initial trial w/public speaking, free assessments & special events.

**Technology/
Internet**   Use Internet for awareness, credibility, delivering free reports/newsletters.

**Strategic
Alliances**   Expand client base by co-marketing w/ CPAs & Estate Planning Attorneys.

Prospecting   Use special events to cross/up-sell existing clients; attract new clients.

Administration   Minimize personal time on admin thru the use of virtual assistant & smart technology.

Bend the Curve
Strategy and Plan Development

We call this exercise, Bend the Curve.

Step 1: Draft an Income, Revenue or Production Objective for the next 1, 3 or 5 years.
Step 2: Brainstorm up to four Strategies that are necessary to achieve the Objective in Step 1.
Step 3: Identify 2 to 4 key Action Plans per Strategy. Action Plans are typically Projects or Programs.

Increase _____ from _____ to _____ by _____.

(Example: Increase total income from $300,000 to $500,000 by 12/31/2014.)

Strategy

Strategy

Strategy

Strategy

Action Plans

_____   _____   _____   _____

_____   _____   _____   _____

_____   _____   _____   _____

Crafting Your Strategies

Listed below are Strategies that are common in the financial services industry. The templates are designed to help you quickly create a first draft.

Customer

Positioning
Become locally/nationally/internationally known for _____.

Target Market
Focus on serving _____, _____ & _____ clients/communities.

Opportunities
Focus on _____, _____ & _____ trends/opportunities.

Products/Services
Core products/services are _____, _____ & _____.

Initial Meeting
Create interest/demand for initial client meeting by _____, _____ & _____.

Process Improvement

Planning & Execution
Strengthen _____ & _____ processes by _____ & _____.

Marketing/Prospecting
Improve mktg/networking/prospecting effectiveness by _____, _____ & _____.

Closing Ratio
Increase closing ratio by _____, _____ & _____.

Product/Service Delivery
Increase quality/timeliness/accuracy of _____ by _____ & _____.

Business Processes
Increase/improve _____ & _____ processes by _____ & _____.

It is not likely all of these Strategies will be appropriate for your business, but this set of templates should help you focus on how you will build your business... and what will make it successful over time.

Learning & Growth

Professional Development/Designations
Develop/improve _____ & _____ professional skills by _____ & _____.

Technical/Product Knowledge
Expand _____ & _____ tech/product knowledge by _____ & _____.

Personal Productivity
Improve personal productivity by _____, _____ & _____.

Communications & Presentation Skills
Improve communication/presentation skills by _____, _____ & _____.

Technology
Invest in/learn _____ & _____ technologies to improve _____ & _____.

Financial

Rate of Growth
Grow business at _____% by _____, _____ & _____.

Profitability
Assure profitability by _____, _____ & _____.

Expense Control
Control expenses by _____, _____ & _____.

Investment in Your Business
Invest in _____ & _____ to support/improve _____ & _____.

Personal Net Worth/Personal Debt
Commit to improve net worth/decrease debt by _____, _____ & _____.

Sample Strategies for Advisors/Agents...

Here are six sets of strategies, from six very different companies. In these examples there are 6 to 8 strategies that describe the "essence of what will make these companies successful over time."

McKenzie Estate Planning Associates

- Specialize in estate planning design, legal docs & services to persons of over $1 mil net worth.
- Provide training to CPAs, attorneys, financial advisors & life insurance agents.
- Restrict Bob McKenzie to professional services and delegate office operations.
- Obtain services of marketing person to sign up professionals for classes.
- Attend professional programs to be up-to-date in field.
- Use technology to maintain both offices & deliver state-of-art estate plans & documents.
- Attract and retain key employees by paying above average salaries and bonuses.

Tri-Valley Financial Advisory Services

- Focus on executing plan, frequent client contact, reviewing markets & client data.
- Capitalize on current clients, and planning and development of trends/opportunities.
- Attract new clients by consistently soliciting referrals in current BOB.
- Positive daily actions are focusing on contacts with clients, reduce administrivia.
- Increase face time with personalized mail campaigns, notes & flawless follow-up.
- Gather AUM by returning to my entire client list for additional assets each quarter.
- Grow assets by closing top 10 referral prospects I have on a monthly basis.

Family Wealth Counselors

- Focus on small business retirement, non-profit endowment & high net worth markets.
- Attract/solicit high net worth thru golf club, non-profit and close personal network.
- Minimize account transfer threats by improved customer service & relationship mgmt.
- Utilize sales and marketing asst. to boost business; increase face time, improve image.
- Pattern business after successful Financial Advisors thru study/observation/interaction.
- Attract new clients thru mail and calling campaigns and persistent follow-up.

and Field Leaders/Executives/Owners

These strategies describe business models, best practices, culture and personal preferences. All were initially created with the fill-in-the-blank templates and then edited. Note that each strategy fits on a single line.

Portland Insurance Agency

- Become locally known for excellence in "family & business insurance solutions".
- Build long term relationships w/ prominent bus. leaders - create consistent referral source.
- Maximize visibility by serving on community, non-profit, & prof boards. Motto: Give Back Often!
- Mine existing client base for "A" clients; use seminar marketing system to find "B"clients.
- Strategic Mktg Alliances - selectively align w/ CPAs, attorneys, auto dealers, real estate profs.
- Sell thru education; use computer presentations to assure consistent message delivery.
- Staffing - hire professionals, provide quality training, 1:1 mentoring, track perf, reward Winners.

Southeast Employee Benefits Group

- Become known for preventing catastrophic employee problems that destroy businesses.
- Attract clients with 50 to 500 employees, business owners who want preventive solutions.
- Promote initial trial through monthly employer council meetings & low-cost guide books.
- Generate revenues thru preventive audits & assessments, training programs & consulting.
- Use technology/Internet for tele-classes, audits & assessments & selling training guides.
- Strategically align our firm w/ local employment law attorneys, CPAs & business consultants.
- Continue to create books, guides, audiotapes & assessment products from existing services.
- Build a business that is ultimately not dependent on my presence; making it saleable.

Tulsa Risk & Insurance Services

- Leverage client and COI relationships for new business referrals to ICP prospects.
- Est. performance team via execution & accountability w/ AEs, Stews, MAA, & Claims.
- Develop suspect COIs w/Continuous Contact COI Strategy Plan (CCCOISP).
- Grow business by asking for & working w/ICP clients.
- Ask every suspect COI for "test case or diagnostic" app w/ their clientele.
- Use direct mail for access to Top 50 prospects and large homes in target market.
- Confirm value and ask for referrals from clients at every meeting.
- Follow up w/ AE and Prospects on open cases weekly.

VISION
MISSION
OBJECTIVES
STRATEGIES
ACTION PLANS

Action Plans

Defining the Work to be Done

Action Plans define the actual work to be done... the specific actions the business must take to implement Strategies and to achieve the Objectives.

For your financial practice, Action Plans will be major business-building or infrastructure projects. They will undoubtedly focus on the execution of your sales, marketing, technology, practice management and productization projects. These projects may require capital and expense budgets; for sure they will consume your valuable time, and may take multiple months to complete.

In well-written One Page Business Plans, Action Plans are NEVER "job description tasks."

Ideally, each Action Plan statement relates to an Objective or a Strategy... but it is not necessary to write an Action Plan for every Objective or Strategy in your One Page Business Plan. You will not have enough space... and more importantly you will not have enough time or money to execute all of the projects you can dream up. Your One Page Plan will accommodate up to nine major Action Plans. We suggest you craft no more than two Action Plans per quarter. For smaller practices – one major project, like developing and implementing a seminar program – may be all that is reasonable to accomplish in one year.

Remember: Your One Page Business Plan is designed to capture the most important elements of your plan... not all of the elements. If you find that nine Action Plans are not enough, it's possible you may need to write a separate One Page Plan for one or more of the larger projects... or more likely, you have defined too many projects for this year.

"Work" may be defined three ways:

- Major business-building projects
- Significant infrastructure projects
- Programs/Projects that bend the curves and/or trend lines

A Simple Formula for Writing Action Plans...

Description of Work + Completion Date = Plan

Here are some examples using the formula:

- Purchase and install contact management software by January 31st.
- Launch 2nd quarter Family Wealth informational seminar series April 20th.
- Complete re-design of web site with e-commerce capabilities by July 31st.
- Complete automation of personalized estate planning presentation by October 31st.
- Hire part-time administrative assistant by February 28th; Bookkeeper by April 30th.

Work "Bends" the Curve... Project Prioritization

In the Strategy section we used the "Bend the Curve" visual to identify the major opportunities that have the potential to significantly grow your business over the next 3 to 5 years. We can again use this visual model to help identify and prioritize the major projects and programs you and your team are going to focus on in the next twelve months.

When you have agreed on the projects that will bend the curve, assign completion dates and responsibility... then craft the Action Plans. Each of these projects is a potential candidate for your One Page Business Plan! Also be sure to calculate the expense and capital budgets for these projects and get them into your One Page Budget Worksheet, which is included in the Financial Services Tool Kit CD.

Identify 2 to 4 projects or programs you are going to implement this year that have the greatest potential for Bending the Curve(s) in your financial practice. You might have a Bend the Curve worksheet for revenue production, commissions or assets under management. Or you might just have one for the entire company. Remember: keep it simple. If a little is good, more does not necessarily make it better.

Increase _____ from _____ to _____ by _____.

(Example: Increase assets under management from $46 to $100 million by 12/31/2014 (3 yr goal).

Project D

Project C

Project B

Project A

Resources Required: People, Expense Budget, Capital Budget

_____   _____   _____   _____

_____   _____   _____   _____

_____   _____   _____   _____

The One Page Planning Wheel

The One Page Planning Wheel is another visual tool that helps visualize key projects over the entire year.

Most people have little problem identifying critical tasks and near-term projects that need to be completed in the next six days... or six weeks. But the identification, prioritization and calendaring of significant projects and programs in the second half of the year... or beyond, can be difficult when the focus is so often on short term results.

Use The One Page Planning Wheel as a tool to brainstorm the key projects for your practice, brand, district, division, company, departments or programs. In the brainstorming phase, identify all major projects, then refine the list down to two or three projects per quarter.

Remember, your One Page Business Plan can accommodate up to nine Action Plans.

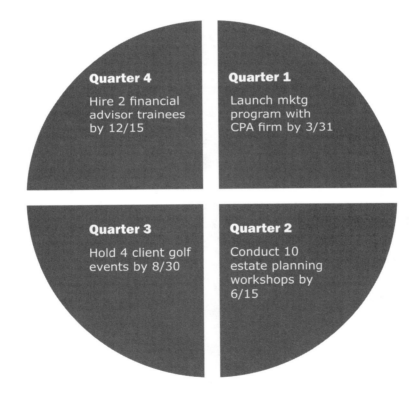

There are four quarters in a year. List one or two major business-building projects that must be accomplished in each of the next four quarters in order to implement your Strategies and achieve your Objectives. When complete, type your Action Plans into The One Page Business Plan template that is in the Financial Services Tool Kit CD.

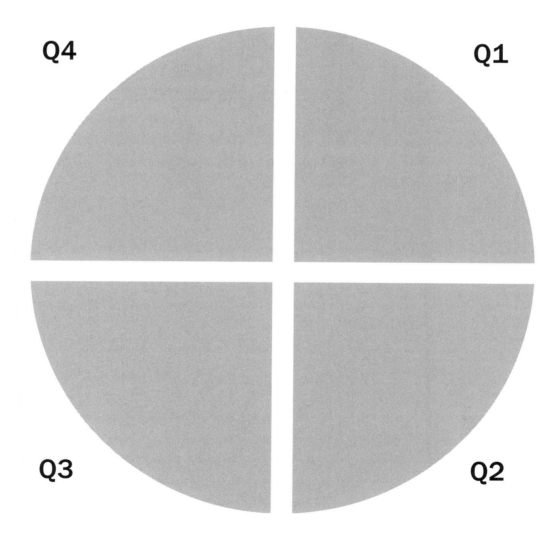

Remember: Time exists so that you do not have to do everything at once.

■ VISION
■ MISSION
■ OBJECTIVES
■ STRATEGIES
■ ACTION PLANS

Assembling and Polishing the Plan

"Congratulations! Your Plan is Now in Writing... What's Next?"

Assemble Your Plan onto One Page!

Select one of The One Page Business Plan templates from the Financial Services Tool Kit CD and type in each of the five elements of the plan you created using the various exercises.

Step Back and Review Your Plan

How does it look to you? If you are like most people, some parts of your plan will be complete, while other parts will still need editing and additional detail. Don't rush the process! Make the obvious changes now, but allow some time to reflect on your plan.

Carry the plan with you; it's only one page! As new ideas and insights appear, capture them on paper. Review the Polishing and Edit suggestions on the next page. Most people find it takes about three drafts to get their plans in solid shape... don't cut the process short. Too much depends on it.

Review Your Plan with Others

You have a plan... now review it with your partners, team, and/or trusted advisors. Have them ask you clarifying questions. Take good notes on the feedback; you might consider recording the feedback sessions. Update your plan with the feedback you decide is appropriate.

Have Partners? Employees? Have them Create their One Page Business Plan

Executives, managers and employees are expensive! After you have reviewed your plan with your team, and they have had a chance to ask clarifying questions, give them 3 to 7 business days to create their One Page Business Plan. Encourage them to work together; the plans will be more cohesive as a result. Have partners? Encourage them to create their plan, then meet to review and compare plans. Make appropriate changes to bring them into alignment.

Balance and Align the Plans

Balancing the plans is a process that ensures all of the functions within your company will be working together, on the right projects and programs, in the proper sequence, at the right time... and not at cross purposes.

When your organization's plans are balanced and aligned... you can have everyone, literally, working on the same page!

Editing and Polishing the Plan

Here is a list of ideas and tips to polish your plan:

Overall Review

- Does your Vision Statement describe what you are building?
- Will your Mission Statement attract new clients? Drive employee behavior? Is it memorable?
- Are your Objectives measurable, dated and graphable?
- Do your Strategies describe what will make your business successful over time?
- Are your Action Plans significant business-building projects? Will they achieve your Objectives?

Order and Abbreviation

- Edit Objectives, Strategies, and Action Plan statements to one line.
- Eliminate all unnecessary words and phrases.
- Abbreviate words when necessary.
- Use symbols like "&" in lieu of "and" to save space.
- Use "k" or "m" for thousands and "M" for millions.
- Communicate priority of Objectives, Strategies, and Action Plans by placing them in the proper order.

Creative Considerations

- Use bullets to make key points stand out.
- Highlight key phrases in italics.

Strengthening Exercises

- Edit Vision, Mission and Strategy until they are enduring statements that "resonate"!
- Drop low-priority items. Remember, "less can produce more."
- Refine Objectives and Action Plans to be specific, measurable, and define accountability.

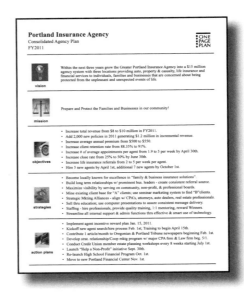

Involve Others

- Few people can write a solid plan by themselves; ask others for feedback.
- Ask your reviewers:
  - Is this plan really strategic? Too optimistic? Too pessimistic?
  - Does it include all of the critical initiatives I have been talking about?
  - Is it too risky? Too safe?
  - Does it reflect my best thinking?
  - What have I overlooked? What do you see that I missed?
- Listen to the feedback, take notes, and ask clarifying questions.
- Revise and update plan for feedback.
- Ask for another round of feedback.
- Most people find it takes at least three drafts to have a solid plan.
- Repeat until you and your reviewers agree it is solid.

Resources, Timelines and Budgets

Having a plan is critical to your success. Here are a few thoughts on other important processes that will help assure your success.

Define the Required Resources

Every project, program and initiative in your plan will need resources... or it will not happen. For each project identify the people, expenses, capital budget and any other resources required to fully execute the plan. The process of identifying the resources may cause you to realize you may not have the capability or capacity of implementing the plan you just wrote. If that is the case, go back and revise the plan.

Project Timelines

Review your project start and completion dates. Are they realistic? One of the major problems with all planning processes is the tendency to think we can do more than we actually can. When we complete a major project or initiative... we feel smart! When we have a list of projects that we have not started or are half done... we feel defeated. Take another hard look at your projects for this next year... would you be extraordinarily pleased if you completed just one or two of them? If so, adjust your plan.

Alignment with Partners & Team

If you have partners or a team, it is not unusual to find during the alignment process that the business units within your company contributing to projects and programs will not have consistent and appropriate start and completion times. For each major project or program, create an overall timeline to assure all of the sub-tasks are in alignment with the overall milestones. If project dates get changed... be sure to update the plans accordingly.

Create a Budget

Almost every activity in a business has a stream of revenue or expenses associated with it. Use your One Page Business Plan(s) to help identify all of the sources of revenue, expense and capital. If you need help in budgeting, get it. This is an important part of your success. Included in the Financial Services Tool Kit CD is a simple One Page Budget Worksheet that should be helpful.

Recommendation: If a practice, department, project, program or company is big enough for a One Page Business Plan, it should have a separate budget.

Implementation... Tracking & Measuring the Plan

Implement Your Plan

Many plans fail because they never get implemented! When great ideas sit on the shelf... nothing happens. Put your plan to work. You can bet your competitors are working on theirs!

Monitor & Measure

Create a Performance Scorecard for each Objective. Remember: Objectives, if well written, must have a numeric value that is graphable. Included in the Financial Services Tool Kit CD is a fun and easy template for creating Scorecards. You can graph your results against your Objectives, Last Year and Forecast (if appropriate)... you will have a visual picture of all the key metrics in your company. It is very simple and easy to determine if you are ahead of target... or behind.

Monthly Business Review

Recent surveys indicate only 1 in 5 businesses have a regularly scheduled monthly business review meeting to monitor the implementation and execution of their plans.

The monthly business review is a fabulous opportunity to learn what really happens in your business each month. Do a quick review of each of the major projects... are they on track? If not, address the issues and define solutions to get them back on track.

Have a business coach, professional advisor, mentor? Make it a practice to schedule an hour with them each month to review your progress against your plan.

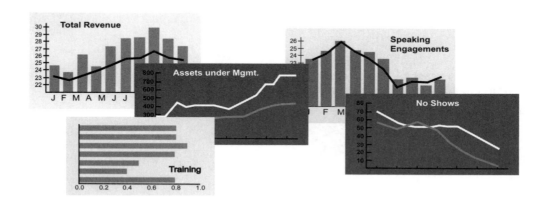

Filling in the Gaps

The process of writing a business plan, in some ways, is like writing a term paper on your business. You capture in writing what you know, conduct research to fill in the gaps, interview knowledgeable people, draft your document, ask for feedback, and then complete the final editing.

Your knowledge of your business is significant. Capture your initial thoughts in the first draft, and then begin the process of reflecting on your plan... and involving others. Keep in mind, the process of planning is one of continual reflection and refinement... and in many ways this is more important than the final document.

Most people have more resources instantly available to them than they realize. These resources are very knowledgeable... and frequently free! They know you, your business, the industry, may share the same clients and may buy from the same vendors.

Resources readily available to you include your team, peer advisors and managers, field trainers and leaders, senior executives, vendors, bankers, attorneys, CPAs, and other financial advisors.

Other significant resources are the national associations. They exist to gather and disseminate information about your industry. They follow all of the trends, innovations, opportunities, regulations, etc. Check out their web sites, better yet pick up the phone and talk with one of the executives. Get to know the regular contributors.

One of the benefits of The One Page Business Plan is that it can be read in less than five minutes. Share your plan with your resources. Invite their insights and feedback. Your plan will be stronger!

"Your Plan is not finished until it represents the best of your thinking!"

Sample Plans...

For some, the easiest way to learn how to write a plan is to take a look at how others have written their plans. In this section we have provided several sample plans for your review.

As you review these plans, you will note that they all follow the One Page Methodology fairly closely... but not necessarily... precisely. That's OK! Each of these plans is a real plan, written by an advisor, agent, field leader, sales executive, managing partner or agency owner. Their personal style comes through! It should... this is their business.

Note: Sample plans have these consistent characteristics

• Vision Statements paint a graphical picture of what is being built.

• Mission Statements are short, most are 8 words or less.

• Objectives are always graphable!

• Strategies describe how the financial practice or company will be built.

• Action Plans describe the work to be done... all have completion dates.

*Sample plans are real plans, but the authors requested their names, company names and locations be altered to protect their privacy.

Portland Insurance Agency

Consolidated Agency Plan

FY2011

vision

Within the next three years grow the Greater Portland Insurance Agency into a $15 million agency system with three locations providing auto, property & casualty, life insurance and financial services to individuals, families and businesses that are concerned about being protected from the unpleasant and unexpected events of life.

mission

Prepare and Protect the Families and Businesses in our community!

objectives

- Increase total revenue from $8 to $10 million in FY2011.
- Add 2,000 new policies in 2011 generating $1.2 million in incremental revenue.
- Increase average annual premium from $500 to $550.
- Increase client retention rate from 88.35% to 91%.
- Increase # of average appointments per agent from 1.9 to 5 per week by April 30th.
- Increase close rate from 25% to 50% by June 30th.
- Increase life insurance referrals from 2 to 5 per week per agent.
- Hire 5 new agents by April 1st, additional 7 new agents by October 1st.

strategies

- Become locally known for excellence in "family & business insurance solutions".
- Build long term relationships w/ prominent bus. leaders - create consistent referral source.
- Maximize visibility by serving on community, non-profit, & professional boards.
- Mine existing client base for "A" clients; use seminar marketing system to find "B"clients.
- Strategic Mkting Alliances - align w/ CPA's, attorneys, auto dealers, real estate professionals.
- Sell thru education; use computer presentations to assure consistent message delivery.
- Staffing - hire professionals, provide quality training, 1:1 mentoring, reward Winners.
- Streamline all internal support & admin functions thru effective & smart use of technology.

action plans

- Implement agent incentive reward plan Jan. 15, 2011.
- Kickoff new agent search/hire process Feb. 1st; Training to begin April 15th.
- Contribute 1 article/month to Oregonian & Portland Tribune newspapers beginning Feb. 1st.
- Develop strat. relationship/Coop mktg program w/ major CPA firm & Law firm beg. 5/1.
- Conduct Credit Union member estate planning workshops every 8 weeks starting July 1st.
- Launch "Help a Non-Profit" initiative Sept. 30th.
- Re-launch High School Financial Program Oct. 1st.
- Move to new Portland Financial Center Nov. 1st.

Tri-Valley Financial Advisory Services

George Rask, CFP

FY2011

vision

By year-end 2013, grow George Rask, at Tri-Valley Advisory Services, into a $350,000 financial advisory service practice managing 40,000,000 in assets, providing trusted financial planning to 30 to 60 year-old clients for their retirement, and for their family's future wealth, who live in the greater Phoenix metro area.

mission

We help families provide for their families!

objectives

- Achieve 2011 production growth of 33%. Grow from $150,000 to $200,000.
- Boost return on assets from 0.20% to 0.40%.
- Increase assets from $21 million to $28 million.
- Maintain the same number accounts while culling lowest 10% of accounts from my BOB.
- Achieve asset-based revenue of 70% of BOB.
- Decrease transaction-based revenue from 38% to 30%.

strategies

- Focus on executing plan, frequent client contact, reviewing markets & client data.
- Capitalize on current clients, and planning and development of trends/opportunities.
- Attract new clients by consistently soliciting referrals in current BOB.
- Positive daily actions are focusing on contacts with clients, reduce administrivia.
- Increase face time with personalized mail campaigns, notes & flawless follow-up.
- Gather AUM by returning to my entire client list for additional assets each quarter.
- Grow assets by closing top 10 referral prospects I have on a monthly basis.

action plans

- Cull 10% of my accounts 2/15.
- Complete retraining on Financial Planning (CFP exam) by 3/15.
- Employ regular use of BIS beginning no later than 4/15.
- Utilize "Financial Planning System" for my top 10% clients beginning 6/15.
- Perform mid-year course correction, and revise business plan as necessary by 6/30.

Family Wealth Counselors, Inc.

Allen Johnson, Financial Advisor

FY2011

---

vision

Within the next three years (YE 2013) grow Allen Johnson, Financial Advisor at Family Wealth Counselors to $75,000,000 in Assets Under Management, with revenues of $700,000 by providing consultative financial services in the greater San Diego area to truly compatible clients consisting of busy professionals, active retirees, non-profit organizations and small to medium businesses.

---

mission

Take complexity out of family wealth.

---

objectives

- Increase 2011 gross revenue from $207,000 to $315,000.
- Grow AUM from $32.7 million to $45 million.
- Boost my ROA from .59 to .70 BPS.
- Eliminate all $0-$35k households clients by 6/30.
- Expand +$100k households clients from 51 to 80.

---

strategies

- Focus on small business retirement, non-profit endowment & high net worth markets.
- Attract/solicit high net worth thru golf club, non-profit and close personal network.
- Minimize account transfer threats by improved customer service & relationship mgmt.
- Utilize sales and marketing asst. to boost business; increase face time, improve image.
- Pattern business after successful Financial Advisors thru study/observation/interaction.
- Attract new clients thru mail and calling campaigns and persistent follow-up.

---

action plans

- Complete training and implementation of SMART! database for myself and CSA by EOY.
- Launch 2 aggressive campaigns per quarter to clients and prospects alike.
- Close 6 small biz retirement plans at rate of 1 every other month; beg. 1/15
- Hold 5 successful golf events for clients; May, June, July, Aug, Sept.
- Complete 12 non-profit endowment presentations by 6/15. 12 more by 12/15.
- Hold weekly Rookie FA business planning meetings for this branch; beg 5/1.

Tulsa Risk & Insurance Services

Susan McNalley

Four Month Plan

---

vision

In the next four months (Sept - Dec) grow my Tulsa PCS practice into a $12K/month revenue generating business specializing in personal P&C sales to high net worth individuals.

---

mission

Create peace of mind through proactive personal risk management.

---

objectives

- Achieve 2011 sales of $100,000.
- Work with prospects greater than or equal to $15K ICP 90% of the time.
- Call 35 prospects by Oct 31st.
- Implement suspect COI strategy w/ 114 suspect COIs in my database 9/1/11 to 1/1/12.
- Produce minimum of $12K in revenue every month in 2011; target $150,000.

---

strategies

- Leverage client and COI relationships for new business referrals to ICP prospects.
- Est. performance team via execution & accountability w/ AEs, Stews, MAA, & Claims.
- Develop suspect COIs w/Coninuous Contact COI Strategy Plan (CCCOISP)
- Grow business by asking for & working w/ICP clients.
- Ask every suspect COI for "test case or diagnostic" app w/ their clientele.
- Use direct mail for access to Top 50 prospects and large homes in target market.
- Confirm value and ask for referrals from clients at every meeting.
- Follow up w/ AE and Prospects on open cases weekly.
- Put all suspect COIs thru CCCOISP.

---

action plans

- Direct mail to large SGV homes by 9/30.
- Client-Confirm Value: ask 4 referrals 2 prospects/COIs.
- Mail letters and f-u by phone to Top 50 by Oct 15th.
- Mail /in-person (CCCOISP) 6 to 7 pre-determined items throughout year based on A,B, or C.
- Dial 114 suspect COIs by Nov 15th.

McKenzie Estate Planning Associates

Bob McKenzie

FY2011 Consolidated Plan

---

vision

Become premiere mid-tier estate planning attorney in Central Valley Counties with offices in Sacramento and Fresno operating in collaboration with selected law firms, CPAs, Life Insurance Agents, Stock Brokers, and other Financial Advisors.

---

mission

We help create, preserve and utilize family wealth for important social causes.

---

objectives

- Produce annual gross of $480,000 and net of $240,000.
- Be retained by two new clients a month at average fee of $20K each.
- Conduct 10 class sessions by 12/31/11 with average attendance of 10 prof @ $25 each.
- Conduct 40 class sessions in 2012 with average attendance of 10 prof @ $25 each.
- Co-conduct 2 seminars by 12/31/11 with CPA's clients on Advanced Est Plan.
- Co-conduct 4 seminars by 2012 with CPA's clients on Advanced Est Plan.
- Obtain 4 qualified Ad Est Plan referrals from Profs with conversion ratio of 50%.
- Obtain 1 qualified Ad Est Plan referral from clients with conversion ratio of 50%.
- Maintain $150,000/year of existing client base practice.

---

strategies

- Specialize in estate planning design, legal docs & services to persons of over $1 mil net worth.
- Provide training to CPAs, attorneys, financial advisors & life insurance agents.
- Restrict Bob McKenzie to professional services and delegate office operations.
- Obtain services of marketing person to sign up professionals for classes.
- Attend professional programs to be up-to-date in field.
- Use technology to maintain both offices & deliver state-of-art estate plans & documents.
- Attract and retain key employees by paying above average and bonus.

---

action plans

- Develop CPA Est & Gift Tax class-get it approved for CE 8 hrs credit by 8/31.
- Teach 2 CPA Est Plan classes by 11/30.
- Get Life Ins Est Plan class reapproved CE credit for 10 hours by 9/30.
- Teach 2 Life Ins Est Plan classes by 12/15.
- Develop Est Planning Mktg 4 hour class for Fin Advisors by 10/30.
- Teach 2 attorney classes by 12/15.
- Develop Est & Gift Tax class for attys by 10/30.
- Teach 2 attorney classes by 12/15.

Financial Advisors Best Practices, Inc.

James McIntire, President

FY2011 Business Plan

ONE
PAGE
PLAN

vision

Within five years, become nationally known author, publisher, speaker and consultant serving independent financial advisors. Consult primarily in greater Boston metro area; approximately 30% of my time. Create products (books, CDs) for the financial advisor market 25% of my time. Speak extensively regionally, building to national recognition. By 2013 total revenues will be $500,000 or more.

mission

We help financial advisors build successful and sustainable practices!

objectives

- Generate total revenues of $175,000 in FY2011.
- Achieve profit before tax of $90,000 in FY2011.
- Increase active consulting client base from 20 to 30; increase consulting fees to $90k.
- Secure 12 paid speaking engagements in at average fee of $2,500.
- Sell 1,000 books in FY11; 25m in FY12, 50m in FY13; 100m in FY14.
- Train 10 registered/certified Practice Advisors by 12/3/11; 100 by 12/31/12.
- Complete best practice CD by 8/31; sell 500 tapes yielding $5,000.
- Complete Advisors Best Practice book by 12/31 – sell 500 copies in FY12.

strategies

- Collaborate to complete; can't do this by myself… Always keep it simple!
- Use personal contacts to create opportunities to speak, get reviews, articles published.
- Self publish to start, prove marketability, seek national publisher.
- Create products & programs for others to sell that serve the advisor market.
- Seek endorsement/approval/intros; Quotes from noted authors, CEOs, SBA.
- Build national brand & corporate identity.
- Exit strategy; sell to major publisher or business training company in 5-7 years.

action plans

- Complete Financial Advisor marketing book by April 30th; print 6,000 copies by May 31st.
- Publish article in GAMA Journal, June/July Issue.
- Develop publicity & marketing plans by 3/31.
- Develop Practice Advisor Certification program by 7/31.
- Contract w/Audio Design Productions for CD production by 7/31.
- Submit articles to 10 major professional finance magazines for December publication.
- Complete mailing to 50 trade associations by 8/31 for speaking engagements.

■ VISION
■ MISSION
■ OBJECTIVES
■ STRATEGIES
■ ACTION PLANS

More Sample Plans

Undoubtably many of your clients are entrepreneurs, executives and business owners. They are building and running everything from micro and main street businesses to mid-market companies to global enterprises. We conservatively estimate over 250,000 of these businesses have created clear, concise plans for growth and profitability.

We thought it would be valuable for you to see how flexible The One Page Business Plan process is by providing you with a wide range of examples. Also by reviewing these plans you may pick up ideas that you can use in your plan.

Have clients that are frustrated with their planning processes? Outgrown their current business plan? Have employees that are working on the wrong projects or programs? Need to develop the next generation of executives or managers to run the business when they retire? Feel free to share some of these sample plans with them, it may be just what they need to get unstuck.

We also included sample non-profit plans. We estimate over the last thirteen years over 5,000 executive directors have successfully written One Page Business Plans for their non-profit.

Colorado Garden Window Company

Mike Bozman, CEO

FY2011 Consolidated Plan

vision

Within the next 3 years grow Colorado Garden Window Company into a $40 million national home products company specializing in manufacturing and distributing custom and replacement garden windows and skylights to baby-boomers and home remodelers.

mission

Bring Light, Air, and the Beauty of Nature into homes… through creative windows!

objectives

- Achieve 2011 sales of $17 million.
- Earn pre-tax profits in 2011 of $1.5 million.
- Target Cost of Goods Sold at 38% of sales.
- Reduce inventory levels to 3.3 months on hand by August 31.
- Grow Garden Window Division at 8% per year & achieve $5.3M this year.
- Expand skylight/custom window product lines; grow sales to $7.5 million this year.
- Implement profit improvement programs & reduce product costs to 38%.
- Achieve 98% on time delivery with 98% order accuracy by 1st quarter.

strategies

- Focus on new upscale home developments and baby-boomer remodeling trends.
- Build Colorado Garden Window Co. into a nationally recognized brand name.
- Control quality processes by manufacturing solely in-house.
- Become vendor-of-choice by maintaining a constant inventory of standard window sizes.
- Increase capacity & manufacturing efficiency by actively reducing duplicate products.
- Centralize distribution into one location; reducing costs & improving service.

action plans

- Introduce new scenic Garden Window at S.F. products show 3/15.
- Roll out new package design beginning April 1.
- Expand Sales Dept. to focus on Signature Homes in Denver and Provo by 4/15.
- Introduce inventory reduction program company-wide by 5/15.
- Fully implement new MRP software to achieve inventory reduction by 7/1.
- Complete skylight product rationalization program by 8/15.
- Research, design and roll out re-designed employee benefit program by 10/1.
- Complete product distribution consolidation project by 11/15.

The HR Consulting Group

Sally McKenzie & Bob Wilson

FY2011 Consolidated Plan

ONE
PAGE
PLAN

---

vision

Within the next 3 years grow The HR Consulting Group into a $1 million North Texas consulting and training company specializing in human resource training and consulting services for companies within a 50 mile radius of Dallas/Ft. Worth that have between 50 and 500 employees.

---

mission

Bring Preventative HR Programs to Growing Companies!

---

objectives

- Achieve 2011 sales of $ 350,000.
- Earn pre-tax profits of $75,000; after paying two partner salaries of $100,000.
- Consistently have partners bill out 6 days per month at $1,500 per day.
- Generate $40,000 from audits & assessments.
- Increase training program & product revenue from $7,500 a month to $10,000 by Aug. 30th.
- Increase ave. bi-weekly attendance at employer council meetings from 12 to 20 by May 15th.
- Produce six notable, publishable case studies in 2011.
- Take a minimum of 2 one-week vacations in the next twelve months.

---

strategies

- Become known for preventing catastrophic employee problems that destroy businesses.
- Attract clients with 50 to 500 employees, business owners who want preventive solutions.
- Promote initial trial through our monthly employer council meetings & low-cost guide books.
- Generate revenues thru preventive audits & assessments, training programs & consulting.
- Use technology/Internet for tele-classes, audits & assessments, & selling training guides.
- Strategically align our firm w/ local employment law attorneys, CPAs & business consultants.
- Continue to create books, guides, audiotapes, & assessment products from existing services.
- Build a business that is ultimately not dependent on my presence; which will make it saleable.

---

action plans

- Publish "Employer's Bill of Rights Handbook" by Feb. 28th.
- Complete Sexual Harassment, Family Leave & Diversity Guidebooks by April 20th.
- Launch "New Manager Training Series" May 1st; repeat program once in Q3 & Q4.
- Begin hosting monthly "Managers Problem Solving Roundtable" in July.
- Complete makeover of web site & e-commerce systems by Sept. 30th.
- Introduce Smart System's web-employee appraisal process to our clients starting Nov. 1st.

ZXM Automation Consulting, Inc.

Allen Marcus, President

FY2011 Consolidated Plan

vision

Within the next five years build ZXM Automation into the premier west coast industrial process automation consulting company specializing in integration solutions. ZXM Automation revenues will grow from $10 million in 2010 to $20 million by 2015 by expanding its role from a manufacturing representative company to a complete engineering field service and process solutions company.

mission

Helping you control your marketing, sales, service and distribution channels!

objectives

- Grow business 20% & achieve total sales revenues of $12 million in 2011.
- Achieve profit before tax of $1 million.
- Land at least 5 significant system projects at a minimum of $250k each in 2011.
- Increase gross margin from 17% to 20%.
- Increase sales per employee from $320,000 to $375,000.
- Increase Engineering Services billable utilization from 50% to 70%.

strategies

- Sell total solutions not parts.
- Significantly increase valued added engineering & integration service capabilities.
- Expand geographically into So. Calif., Oregon/Washington, Nevada, Arizona, Alaska.
- Aggressively target niche markets in each geographic market.
- Expand thru selective acquisitions and/or strategic partnerships.
- Continually develop the discipline of profitability for ZXM & our clients.
- Attract/retain key employees by maximizing their creative, technical & business talents.
- Share growth & prosperity w/ employees through incentive & equity participation

action plans

- Critical Marketing Program: Visit all 25 base system clients in 2nd Q.
- Hire System Eng. by 4/30 and Sales Mgr. by 6/30.
- Implement Client Awareness & F2K Support Programs in 3rd Q.
- Complete UC Berkeley, Lipton, SAI projects successfully by 9/30.
- Implement F2K Demo website in 4th Q.
- Install new NT server by 3/31 & Unix server in 2nd Q.
- Implement Sales Automation Program and complete conference room demo in 3rd Q.
- Complete business practices, procedures & policy manual by 12/31.

Meals on Wheels

Donna Van Sant, Executive Director

FY2011 Business Plan Summary

vision

Grow Meals On Wheels program into a premier nutrition service for the home bound elderly and disabled adults in our county, providing a full compliment of quality prepared meals and personal attention seven days a week.

mission

At home and healthy with full nutrition and personal attention.

objectives

- Provide services to 475 home bound elderly each month.
- Provide expanded nutritional service products to 300 individuals.
- Add new customers at the rate of 45 per month.
- Increase case management revenue to an average of $2,500 per month.
- Recruit and train 25 new route drivers, both volunteer and paid.
- Obtain $80,000 in county contract and foundation funding.
- Provide 12 in-service training sessions for route drivers and 24 for MoW staff.
- Provide nutrition services to 75 disabled adults each month.

strategies

- Develop and maintain effective relations with funders; program tours, and proposal writing.
- In conjunction with food services vendors, develop three new products for our customers.
- Develop and execute a customer focused marketing plan for nutrition and CS management.
- Create and execute a staff and volunteer development plan that works!
- Operate our customer feedback and quality control system to increase customer satisfaction.

action plans

- Complete new product development by March 23rd.
- Complete staff hiring and support plan by May 16th.
- Hold program tour and meeting with all current funders by October 10th.
- Win funding from 10 new foundations by November 23rd.
- Develop a marketing plan by December 1st.

City of Pageville Fire Department

Robert Lewellyn, Fire Chief

FY2011 Consolidated Plan

ONE
PAGE
PLAN

---

vision

Within the next three years achieve a fire and emergency services team in the City of Pageville that is characterized by high employee morale and excellent community service.

---

mission

Elevate citizen confidence that their fire and emergency services are dependable and affordable. Protecting community with quality life... and fire-safety services.

---

objectives

- Reduce fire response time to 5 minutes average by 12/31.
- Reduce freeway emergency response time to 7 minutes average by 12/31.
- Reduce loss of property by 12% from previous year.
- Assure there is no more than a 5% deviation from last year's monthly overtime budget.
- Reduce worker injuries to no more than 6 per month by 12/31.
- 60% employees involved in participation activities by 7/01.

---

strategies

- Involve community in neighborhood targeted life and safety program.
- Involve all personnel in every aspect of life and fire safety at their locations.
- Establish and enforce performance based accountability system at all department levels.
- Establish and provide professional growth and opportunity programs for all personnel.
- Coordinate with other agencies to meet emergency response standards.
- Deliver safety education & other services within our mission to the community.
- Aggressively work to prevent hazardous conditions.
- Respond promptly to rescues, fires, medical emergencies and natural disasters.
- Ensure safe, professional, environmentally harmonious actions.

---

action plans

- Develop a coordinating mechanism to keep track of all elements of the strategic plan by 3/31.
- Accountability systems are developed for all elements of the strategic plan by 6/1.
- Implementation of the strategic plan is monitored on a monthly basis by 7/31.
- Develop a list of comparable cities and fire departments to benchmark our services by 9/1.
- A commitment plan to guide building of a policy maker consensus on service levels by 10/1.
- Implement a comprehensive employee involvement plan by 10/31.
- Implement a comprehensive community involvement plan by 12/31.

Unity of Marin, Spiritual Center

Reverend Richard Mantei

FY2011 Consolidated Plan

vision

The vision of Unity In Marin is to provide a loving and supportive diverse community which teaches practical Christianity and encourages spiritual growth and action. Within 3 years 700 will attend 3 transformational Sunday services, and a mid-week, and monthly healing service. We will have an active 7-day per week spiritual center and have 100+ children in YE with 40 personal growth and spiritual education class night/events for adults per mo. UIM will have 3 effective outreach programs in Marin County and beyond. People will experience a deep sense of spiritual community, personal transformative growth and service to others as a path to God.

mission

Discover divinity within and reach out in loving service.

objectives

- Increase Sunday attendance from 220 to 400 by December 31.
- Increase annual income from $380,000 to $620,000.
- Increase Y.E. weekly attendance from 15 average to 40 average.
- Increase new membership from 75 to 100, increase AE class 12 to 25 attend 160 to 450.
- Increase Spring and Fall in-home program from 100/150 to 180/220.
- Increase Service Ministry involvement from 105 to 150.

strategies

- Bld upon successful Sunday Celebration: enhance music & pre/post service experience.
- Meet goals of FIA/CC/LegacyEndow/other profit making events thru excellent in execution.
- Bld Edu. success by increased variety/continuity & excel in curric & teachers.
- Deepen prayer consciousness by expanding role of chaplains, outreach and education.
- Bld membership by better marketing & outreach prog.& congreg. involve.
- Bld upon MLT success by inviting/recognizing/ coaching/thanking excellence in leadership.
- Leverage minister's time by evolving staff and leadership teams.

action plans

- In Q1 Complete negotiations & details for 6 nat'l speakers by 1/31.
- In Q1 Complete Sunday, seminar, theme programming for the year by 3/15.
- In Q1 Complete arrangements for once per month healing service.
- In Q2 Finalize plans for a mid-week service to begin in September.
- In Q3 Have 75% of work done in preparation for Capital Campaign launch by 4/30.
- In Q4 Fully implement transition team for YE leadership by 10/31.
- In Q4 By November 30th, complete plans to implement Capital Campaign next year.

Bay Area Entrepreneur Association

George Cole, Executive Director

FY2011 Strategic Plan

vision

Build BAEA into a nationally recognized micro-enterprise organization with an extensive greater San Francisco Bay Area network of entrepreneurial support groups providing nationally recognized products, programs and services to entrepreneurs, small business owners, and partner organizations.

mission

Create viable businesses and successful entrepreneurial leaders through networking, support and connection to resources.

objectives

- Increase membership from 150 to 300 by 12/31/11.
- Launch 2 networks by 6/2011 and add 3 more networks by 6/2012.
- Generate $8,000 from entrepreneurial programs, events and products in FY 2011.
- Host 3 regional network events with at least 50 attendees each and generate $3,000.
- Conduct 4 workshops/programs with an average of 25 participants and generate $4,000.
- Increase low-income members to 25 and increase minority members 25% by 3/2011.
- Award 5 scholarships totaling $1,300 in FY 2011.
- Recognize 10 entrepreneurs for outstanding business growth & community service.

strategies

- Use public relations and media to share successes, educate, recruit and fund.
- Market and sell BAEA endorsed products and services nationally.
- Collaborate with nat'l micro-enterprise org. in nat'l awareness programs and funding.
- Establish BAEA center to create long-term community presence & financial asset base.
- Enlist key community leaders and businesses to launch and develop new networks.
- Attract/retain low-income entrepreneurs by offering scholarships funded by corp. sponsors.
- Utilize multi-lingual/cultural programs to attract minority entrepreneurs.
- Package successful BAEA programs & products to sell to other micro-enterprise orgs.
- Use technology to manage growth, streamline ops., and deliver programs, & sell products.

action plans

- Collect and write 20 success stories by March 15; Implement PR Plan by June 15.
- Complete 5-year Strategic Plan by June 30.
- Launch sales/marketing plan of One Page Business Plan by July 1.
- Complete funding plan by 6/2011. Raise $100,000 by Nov. 30.
- Hire executive director by Sept. 15.
- Expand board of directors from 4 to 7 by Nov. 30.
- Develop BAEA product and service marketing plan by Jan. 2012.
- Develop 2-year network expansion plan by March 2012.

Z-TEC, Inc. – Consolidated Plan

Jerome Johnson, CEO

FY2011 Plan

vision

Within the next three years build Z-TEC, Inc. into a $2 billion global provider of integrated workflow management solutions for Fortune 1000 companies, major municipalities and significant governmental agencies at the country, state, regional and federal level. Z-TEC, Inc. will be headquartered in San Francisco with offices in New York, Dallas, London, Singapore and Rio de Janeiro.

mission

Building Industrial Strength Business Systems!

Our systems improve productivity, and reduce the costs of maintenance, materials, and facilities for large process oriented companies and municipalities.

objectives

- FY2011 Revenue of at least $900 Million.
- FY2011 Profit before Interest & Taxes of $85 Million.
- Complete at least 300 new installations and obtain 500 new clients by EOY 2011.
- Migrate at least 250 existing clients to Z-TEC web product cost reduction program.
- Increase Gross Margin from 51% to 55% through product cost reduction program.
- Increase sales per field employee from $250,000 to $300,000 by 9/30.
- Reduce Accounts Receivables from 60 days to 45 days.
- Achieve FTE head count of 1,500 by 11/30.

strategies

- Growth: Grow 50% each year by development of new clients and migration of existing clients.
- Reputation: Product position & strong reputation from existing client/partner referrals.
- Partnering: Align with industry leaders, partnering for marketing & solution development.
- Competitive Position: Optimize user/based pricing & modular system concepts for flexibility.
- Product Approach: Configure rather than Customize, Business Rules vs. custom programs.
- R&D: WorkFlow Solutions, Open Systems, multiple environments, Object-Oriented, flexible.
- Develop aligned team, know the plan, have sense of urgency, responsibility & accountability.
- Develop Employee Incentive Program to allow the team to share in the rewards & have fun.

action plans

- Implement Power Partner Initiatives w/Oracle UK by 3/31.
- Complete development of the Z-TEC client/server product by 3/31.
- Develop Sales & Marketing Resource Plan by 4/31.
- Develop Partner strategies w/PeopleSoft, Sun Micro, IBM by 4/30.
- Launch Europe Customer Forum in London at June 2011 Convention.
- Develop Sales Force Automation Plan by August, implement in 4th Quarter.
- Implement financial reporting system at project/dept. level by Oct. 31.
- Implement professional skills development program by Nov. 30.

Z-TEC Inc. – Southern European Sales Division

Alex Morgan, Sales Division Mgr.

FY2011 Plan

vision

Within the next three years grow the southern Europe division of Z-TEC into a $150 million business unit with offices in Madrid, Barcelona, Nice and Florence.

mission

Find customers... close contracts!

objectives

- Increase sales to $45 million in FY2011.
- Complete installation of 50 systems in FY2011.
- Increase gross margins from 51 to 55% by increasing sale of value added services.
- Increase contribution margin to $20 million.
- Migrate at least 35 existing clients to Z-TEC internet product by 12/31.
- Reduce accounts receivable from 60 to 45 days.
- Achieve FTE head count of 275 by 9/31.

strategies

- Partners: Align with industry leaders, partnering for marketing & solution development.
- Product Approach: Configure rather than customize business rules vs. custom programs.
- Market Positioning; modular systems for flexibility, customization; premium pricing.
- R&D: Workflow solutions, open systems, multi-platform, object-oriented, flexible.
- Develop an aligned team with sense of urgency, responsibility and accountability.
- Develop employee incentive programs to allow the team to share rewards.

action plans

- Implement Power Partner Initiatives w/Oracle Spain by 5/31.
- Launch European Customer Forum in Spain at June convention.
- Develop Sales Force Automation Plan by 08/31, implement in 4th quarter.
- Implement financial reporting system at project/dept level by 10/31.
- Implement professional skills development program by 11/15.
- Complete Portugal facilities upgrades by 12/15.
- Complete communication & team performance training w/12 branch mgrs. by 3/31.

Z-TEC, Inc. – Project 6782 Printer Memory
Len Waide, Director

FY2011 Product Development Department Plan

vision

Develop economically viable solution to 6782 printer memory error problem by 12/1/11!

mission

Reduce the incidence of printer fatal error messages.

objectives

- Achieve .0000032 per thousand memory errors per average test cycle by Sept 1.
- Keep cost of upgrade to $1.53 per shipped unit.
- Operate within budget of $356,000.

strategies

- Use 3 teams of 2 engineers plus 2 outside consultants.
- Concentrate on fixing current design rather that replacing it with another.
- Hold weekly progress meeting with team to review progress against plan/budget.
- Use outside consultants on as needed basis for new laser technologies.

action plans

- Establish teams by 3/1.
- Identify and qualify 2 outside consultants; finalize contracts by 3/1.
- Complete problem assessment by 5/31.
- Propose an engineering solution by 6/30.
- Complete prototypes by 7/31.
- Complete product trials by 8/30.
- Document final product specs by 9/30.

Z-TEC, Inc. – Controller

Gail French, Controller, European Division

FY2011 Controller's Department Plan

vision

Within the next five years, build an integrated accounting function at Z-TEC that provides complete accounting support services, management & business analysis and budgeting & forecasting to properly support Z-TEC at $2 billion in revenue.

mission

Provide tools & information to manage growth… profitably!

objectives

- Increase gross margins from 38% to 45%.
- Identify and implement $150k in cost saving projects.
- Close and issue monthly financial statements by the 15th of each month by September 30th.
- Reduce Z-TEC accounts receivable from 65 days to 55 days outstanding.
- Pay off line of credit by September 30th.

strategies

- Build a Z-TEC financial services team that can grow with Z-TEC by training/empowerment.
- Build a business mentality by providing training on fin. statements, budgets & forecasting.
- Increase gross profit by creating mgmt. reporting on non-billable time and material.
- Control expense by dept. budgets, use of policy, forecasting system, timely financials.
- Streamline acctg. process w/ operations dept. to minimize month end billing bottlenecks.
- Improve cash flow thru weekly AR collection monitoring and reduce billing errors.
- Streamline the payroll and HR process thru remote data entry and integrated systems.
- Eliminate duplicate data entry/manual reporting by consolidating to one operating system.
- Finance growth thru internal funds and bank debt; control expense/keep margins high.

action plans

- Build initial Financial Reportings, IS, BS, Dept. expense, sales repts. by February 28th.
- Streamline monthly closing procedure by February 28th.
- Train staff in new closing procedure by March 31st; complete job descriptions by April 30th.
- Build Banking System direct deposit to lockbox by Feb 28th.
- Build 2012 budget analysis model by August 31st; finalized by September 30th.
- Investigate new payroll system w/HR systems by October 31st.
- Finished 2012 budget by Dec 15th.

Z-TEC Inc. – Personnel Manager

Jonee Grassi, Personnel Manager

FY2011 Plan

vision

Develop a world class workforce of employees for Z-TEC International and their independent contractors who fuel the growth of the company through their creativity, dedication, and capabilities

mission

Attract, build and retain a world-class team.

objectives

- Recruit 1,600 new employees by EOY; end year with 3,600 employees.
- Decrease turnover rate from 18% to less than 10%.
- Decrease overtime from 22% to 10%.
- Increase average learning program hours/employee to 60 per year.
- Achieve internal promotion rate of 60%.
- Increase flex-scheduling optimization to 90%.

strategies

- Hire world-class team players with exceptional skill sets whenever possible.
- Retain our employees by treating them as strategic partners critical to our success.
- Commit to have resources, people & systems in place before they are needed.
- Ensure career development through innovative training & development programs.
- Highly compensate employees for their contribution; generous use of stock options.
- Support work-life balance through flex scheduling and well-being programs.
- Develop Employee Incentive Programs to allow our team to share in the rewards.

action plans

- Implement Z-TEC Employee Hiring Campaign by 01/15.
- Launch Employee Distance Learning Program by 02/01.
- Develop Intranet Flexible Scheduling facility by 04/30; implement by 9/30.
- Complete national salary survey by 06/31.
- Upgrade Kansas City national training facilities by 06/30.
- Implement professional skills development program by 11/30.

Z-TEC, Inc – Mgmt. Team Development Program

Jerome Johnson, CEO

FY2011 Plan

---

vision

Evolve the existing management team into a vital growing force that:
- Fuels the growth of the company by seeing and being a part of the larger vision.
- Builds on its own energy and successes; and learns from its failures/shortfalls.
- Expands its capacity to contribute to the overall management of the company.
- Develops an esprit de corps that is supportive of the individual, the team, and the company.
- Develops a manufacturing team focused on meeting the needs of the customer.
- Designs a flexible & adaptable work style/culture able to move quickly & profitably.

---

mission

Build a management team that builds the business!

---

objectives

- Improve quality of decision making (measurement TBD).
- Decrease amt of time & effort to achieve mgmt. buy-in on key projects (measurement TBD).
- Reduce average time in management meetings from 25 hours/month to 12.
- Reduce average work week for management from 60 hours to 45 hours.
- Increase internal promotion ratio from 5% to 25%.
- Decrease management turnover from 20% per year to 5%.

---

strategies

- Evolve the management team over time; do not go for immediate quick fix.
- Encourage growth and increased participation, geared to individual learning styles.
- Transfer skills from President to the mgmt. staff; provide training and coaching as needed.
- Raise collective business and financial consciousness of the team by the sharing of info..
- Allow for small errors, learn from all mistakes, and celebrate the successes!
- Minimize fanfare about the process; let team respond to positive, subtle changes.

---

action plans

- Implement business planning and budgeting process for 2012 starting in Nov.
- Design and implement financial reporting system at "level 2" by Jan. 31.
- Implement monthly business review sessions starting Feb. 20.
- Use CGC Consulting Group to facilitate quarterly "development meetings" starting 3/15.
- Implement new manager's training program in June; new supervisor's training in Aug.
- Begin development of new employee orientation learning module in Oct.
- Complete development of new employee orientation learning module by 11/15.

Notes

Final Thought...

 Most of us have no shortage of good ideas! The issue is which ideas are we going to act on?

Learn to say no to "good ideas"... yours, your partners, employees, associates, friends and family. You only have time, money and resources to execute the "great ideas." The great ideas can be written on the back of an envelope. They are memorable! They catalyze people and businesses.

Planning doesn't need to be complex! Keep it simple!

Jim Horan
President
The One Page Business Plan Company

The One Page Business Plan Company

Workshops and TeleClasses

The One Page Business Plan® is available to you, your partners or team or your entire company as a workshop, annual retreat, teleclass or complete planning program. Experienced facilitators will tailor the presentation or facilitation to meet your needs.

All classes and programs are hands-on working sessions designed to teach participants how to write a clear, concise, understandable business plan, on a single page, in the quickest and simplest way possible.

Planning & Performance Management Software

Our innovative web-based system uniquely links The One Page Business Plan with an executive dashboard and a simplified project tracking system. Over the last seven years, companies from small professional service firms to international corporations have benefited from this system.

The system requires no IT support and can be learned in 30 minutes. Interested? The One Page Planning and Performance System is rapidly becoming the planning system of choice.

Professional Certification

We are interested in partnering with experienced business, government, and not-for-profit consultants and coaches. If your firm provides strategic planning and/or performance management consulting services, The One Page Business Plan may be a profitable addition to your toolkit.

Consultants and advisors who successfully complete the training and certification programs will be licensed to market, sell and implement One Page Business Plan products and services.

The One Page Business
Plan Company
1798 Fifth Street
Berkeley, CA 94710
Phone: (510) 705-8400
Fax: (510) 705-8403
jhoran@onepagebusinessplan.com
www.onepagebusinessplan.com

Acknowledgements

This book could not have been created without the incredible work of almost one hundred of our licensed One Page Business Plan consultants who specialize in the field of financial services. These dedicated consultants proved this one-page methodology could indeed serve this highly technical, sophisticated industry. To them I express a deep heartfelt thanks!

To list all of the people who contributed in little and big ways to the creation of this body of knowledge and this book would take pages. However I wanted to personally express my gratitude to the individuals listed below for their creative ideas and suggestions on how to make The One Page Business Plan a truly effective tool for the financial services industry.

Ted Capistrant
George Cutler
Joe Dager
Mark DiNunzio
Ronn Ellis
Linda Fayerweather
Rob Ferguson
Yvonne Kinney Hockert
Bill Hughes

Tom Leal
Chuck Longanecker
Bob Kramer
Pete Krammer
Maria Marsala
Toni Nell
Anne Nelson
Graeme Nichols
Mike Owens

Joyce Paes
Jerry Pinney
Scott Purcell
Diane Ruebling
Keri Stewart
Larry Sveda
Skip Torresson
Ron Wilder

I would like to extend an extra dose of thanks and gratitude to Nick Ray (CLU, RHU, ChFC, MBC) for his help with this book. His 30+ years with Northwestern Mutual Life as a top producer, Life Member - MDRT and Life Member - LPRT provided many important insights.

Financial Services Tool Kit
How to Install and Use the CD

Installation Instructions:

Simply load the CD into your CD drive. requires Microsoft Word® and/or Excel® to use the templates, forms and spreadsheets. Open any Directory with a double-click. Select desired Word® document or Excel® spreadsheet.

CAUTION:

Immediately after opening any of the files we encourage you to save the file with a new name using the "SAVE AS" command in order to preserve the original content of the file.

No Technical Support

This CD is provided without technical or software support. Please refer to your Microsoft Word® or Excel® User Manuals for questions related to the use of these software programs.

System Requirements:

Windows 95/98/NT/2000/XP/Vista
Macintosh OS 9.1 or higher
Microsoft Word® and Excel®
CD/ROM drive